Practical
Fairy Tales
for
Everyday
Living

Revised Second Edition

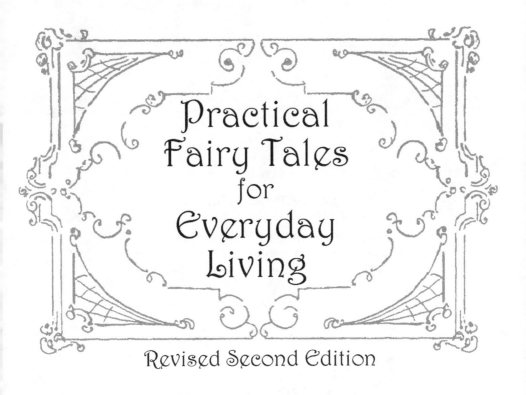

Practical
Fairy Tales
for
Everyday
Living

Revised Second Edition

Martin H. Levinson

INSTITUTE OF GENERAL SEMANTICS

REVISED SECOND EDITION

Cover & Interior Book Design by Scribe Freelance
www.scribefreelance.com

ISBN: 978-0-9860764-2-8 (Paperback)
978-0-9860764-0-4 (eBook)

Published in the United States of America

For Neil Postman

The worlds we manage to get inside our heads are mostly worlds of words.

—Wendell Johnson

OTHER TITLES INCLUDED IN
The New Non-Aristotelian Library Series
Corey Anton, Series Editor

Korzybski, Alfred (2010). *Selections from Science and Sanity.* (2nd Ed.). Edited by Lance Strate, with a Foreword by Bruce I. Kodish. Fort Worth, TX: Institute of General Semantics.

Strate, Lance (2011). *On the Binding Biases of Time and Other Essays on General Semantics and Media Ecology.* Fort Worth, TX: Institute of General Semantics.

Anton, Corey (2011). *Communication Uncovered: General Semantics and Media Ecology.* Fort Worth, TX: Institute of General Semantics.

Levinson, Martin H. (2012). *More Sensible Thinking.* New York, NY: Institute of General Semantics.

Anton, Corey & Strate, Lance (2012). *Korzybski and...* (Eds.) New York, NY: Institute of General Semantics.

Levinson, Martin H. (2014). *Continuing Education Teaching Guide to General Semantics.* New York, NY: Institute of General Semantics.

Berger, Eva & Berger, Isaac. (2014). *The Communication Panacea: Pediatrics and General Semantics.* New York, NY: Institute of General Semantics.

Pace, Wayne. R. (2017). *How to Avoid Making A Damn Fool of Yourself: An Introduction to General Semantics.* New York, NY: Institute of General Semantics.

Lahman, Mary P. (2018). *Awareness and Action: A Travel Companion.* New York, NY: Institute of General Semantics.

Contents

Preface to the Second Edition

I would like to thank readers of the first edition for their many positive comments and particular suggestions leading to revisions. As a reader myself, I also found in rereading the book that there were parts of stories that could be tightened up and improved. With this edition I have tried to do that and hope readers of the first edition, as well as new readers, will enjoy the revised content and general semantics perspectives.

Acknowledgments

I would like to thank Paul D. Johnston, whose illustrations were used in the first edition of this book, for allowing those illustrations to be used in this edition. I would also like to thank the members of the Westhampton Free Library Writers Group for their input on these stories and Donna McGullam, whose expert editing skills have made this a better book. To my wife, Kathy, a fellow writer, I offer special thanks for constantly reminding me that writing is rewriting and that a written work is never finished, only abandoned.

Introduction

The *American Heritage Dictionary* defines the term "fairy tale" as a fictitious, highly fanciful story or explanation. Can such a narrative furnish useful advice on important topics like sound thinking, smart decision-making, stress reduction, emotional self-management, and getting along better with others? This book answers in the affirmative.

Practical Fairy Tales for Everyday Living provides twenty-four whimsical stories featuring characters who successfully battle a variety of personal problems and mishaps through the formulations of general semantics (GS), a science-based "self-help" system designed to assist individuals to better evaluate and solve everyday difficulties and gain a more accurate picture of themselves and the world in which they live.[1] While the stories are not true in the literal sense of that word, the British writer G.K. Chesterton observed, "Fairy tales are more than true—not because they tell us dragons exist, but because they tell us dragons can be beaten."

Some of the stories you will find here contain plot elements from familiar literary classics and children's fairy tales. Others offer completely original scenarios. All the stories have in common a desire to inform and entertain with a bit of humor. That was my purpose in writing these tales and I hope that is your experience in reading them.

---

[1] More information on general semantics can be found at www.generalsemantics.org.

Bucky the Time-Binding Beaver

Once upon a time, in a beguiling little burg near Beaverton, Oregon, there lived a beaver named Bucky who was in the construction business. Bucky's specialty was erecting dams—specifically beaver dams. These barriers help to create the deep water that is needed for winter food storage. Beavers have been putting up dams the same way for thousands of years and they are pretty good at it.

One spring day, Dr. Donald R. Griffin, an American zoology professor and the founder of the field of animal cognition, came to Beaverton. He wanted to capture a beaver and implant a human brain into its skull. Griffin thought beavers were clever critters. He was always telling his students, "When we think of the kinds of animal behavior that suggest conscious thinking, the beaver comes naturally to mind."[1]

Bucky was sitting on a log, happily munching a water lily tuber and flapping his tail, when Griffin and a group of fellow zoological researchers surrounded him. They anesthetized the hapless mammal, put him in a bag, and took him to a laboratory at Oregon State University—the home of the Beavers. In the lab, Griffin surgically

---

[1] This is a real quote from Donald R. Griffin, a real professor of zoology. The experiment in this story is imaginary but stranger things have happened in real life. As Mark Twain said, "Truth is stranger than fiction, but it is because Fiction is obliged to stick to possibilities; Truth isn't."

inserted a human brain into Bucky's head.

When the operation was over, and the anesthetic had worn off, Griffin asked Bucky how he felt. Bucky responded, "I feel a little tired but other than that I feel fine. How did the Beavers do today? Did they beat UCLA?"

Bucky quickly became a highly visible TV talk-show guest, appearing on ABC, NBC, CBS, CNN, FOX, MSNBC, and CSPAN (the latter station featured Bucky's testimony to a Congressional subcommittee on animal rights). In flying around the country to do interviews, Bucky was amazed by the diversity of human architecture that he saw. He discussed his amazement of man-made edifices on CNN with Christiane Amanpour. The following is an excerpt from that show.

Amanpour: What did you do for a living before your brain operation, Bucky?

Bucky: I was in construction, Christiane. Mostly dam building.

Amanpour: How did that work out for you?

Bucky: Not bad. I wasn't the best dam builder in the world but I built some pretty good dams. I took a CNN news crew out to see one of them last week.

Amanpour: What do you think the major difference is between beaver and human structures?

Bucky: I believe the biggest difference is that your species improves its erections with every generation, while beavers keep building the same damn dams.

Amanpour: Alfred Korzybski, the originator of general semantics, had the same thought about human technological progress. He said humans are a *time-binding* class of life. Time-binders use language and other symbols to transmit information across time, which enables each generation to start where the last one left off. He labeled animals a *space-binding* class of life. Space-binders transform energy into movement through space. Space-binders can't convey information over time because they lack language and other forms of communication.

Bucky: I wish my space-binding beaver friends would evolve a little so they could imitate their time-binding human cousins.

Amanpour: Maybe someday they will. In the meantime, because humans possess a quarter of an inch of cortex, our species remains on the top rung of the evolutionary ladder.

Bucky: Well put, Christiane. I like the idea of distinguishing animals from humans on the basis of brain structure.

Amanpour: So did Korzbyski. He came up with the notion that a quarter of an inch of cortex separates animals from human beings. And because I'm a time-binder I was able to read and grasp what he said.

Bucky: Good for you, Christiane, and good for your species! Time-binding has enabled your genus to make countless advances. You've produced the Golden Gate Bridge, personal computers, and rocket ships that can go to the moon. What have beavers done? We're still building your basic beaver dam and beaver lodge.

Amanpour: Buck up, Bucky. You're one of us now. Your ability to use human language has made you a fellow time-binder. Perhaps you should consider relinquishing your beaver identity.

Bucky: I'm not sure I want to do that. While I see the advantages of time-binding in furthering human technology, I don't see similar gains being made in the area of human relations. People fight a lot with each other and with so many atomic weapons around there's a good chance humankind might wipe itself out.

Amanpour: That's a good point. Korzybski also noticed the disparity between the strides humans have made in technology and the lack of progress people have shown in interpersonal interactions. To lessen that gap he came up with general semantics, a theoretical and practical system of critical thinking that involves the use of the scientific method and special language strategies to solve problems of everyday living. It's a pity more folks are not familiar with his work.

Bucky: Maybe I can help to popularize general semantics. I think I'll mention it when I'm on the *PBS News Hour* tonight. I can also put in a plug for general semantics when I appear on *Meet the Press* this weekend. And I will drop a reference to general semantics on *The Voice* next week. I'm singing a song on that show from my new album, *Leave It to Beaver*.

Amanpour: My goodness, you certainly are an eager beaver to get general semantics out to the public.

Bucky: You're right, Christiane; I am. I don't want the planet destroyed because of human stupidity. I want people to cooperate and work on advancing civilization.

Amanpour: That's a noble sentiment, Bucky. Is there anything else you want?

Bucky: I'd like to put up condos and office buildings in New York and Miami. I've had it with building beaver dams. There's just no future in that line of work.

Amanpour: Well, I'll be damned.

Lear with a Schmear

King Dunderhead was a naïve royal who thought people were always honest in their opinions. When the palace chef, who everyone knew hated the king for insisting that steak tartare be cooked and that Chardonnay accompany the royal meatloaf, complimented the monarch for his excellent taste and superior knowledge in the culinary arts, Dunderhead believed him. And when the Prime Minister, who had plotted seven assassination attempts on the king's life, toasted the king's health at royal banquets, he believed him too.

Dunderhead had three daughters—Shirley, Shelly, and Sheba—whom he loved equally well. But they did not all love him in a reciprocal manner. Shirley and Shelly detested their father.

One day, Dunderhead decided that since he was close to the age of mandatory retirement (the rule in the kingdom was that potentates had to exit the throne at age sixty-five) he would divide his realm into three equal parts and give one to each daughter. Dunderhead felt so good about his decision that at dinner that night he had a double portion of grilled steak tartare, smothered with thick mushroom gravy, and a bottle of Thunderbird wine.

At breakfast the next day, Dunderhead announced his plan to bestow on his daughters the royal real estate.

"Oh, pop," Shirley cried, "you are the best father a girl could have. I always sing your praises to my friends and the hangers-on at court.

You rock!"

Shelly was equally gushing in her encomiums for the king and consideration of his welfare. But Sheba remained silent.

"Sheba," the king said, "don't you have anything nice to say to me?"

"You know what's in my heart, Father."

"I want to hear it."

"Look, Dad, when you were sick last April I stayed at your bedside for the ten days you were in the hospital. Shirley and Shelly were around but they were too busy sipping lattés at the Royal Starbucks to visit you. When you asked that one of us girls major in nursing at college, because you wanted a trained family member to minister to your needs in case you became ill in the future, I volunteered to do that. My sisters took up recreation and leisure studies. And when Mom ran away with the Duke of Earl last spring, I remained with you day and night for two months listening to your complaints about the Queen and her paramour and making sure you took the Royal Prozac while my siblings went out clubbing. Actions speak louder than words, Father."

"I am very disappointed in you, Sheba," the king replied. "Your sisters have always held me in the highest regard. They are forever telling me what a fine fellow I am and how they can't wait to take care of me when I retire. You never say those things. I'm beginning to think you don't love me."

"My devotion to you is clear."

"Damn it, Sheba. Are you going to sing my praises or do I take the land I was going to give you and leave it to your sisters instead?"

"The land is yours to do with as you wish," Sheba responded. "I have nothing more to say."

Those words sent the monarch into a royal tizzy. In a state of high dudgeon, he told Sheba, "You are banished from my kingdom! You have till tonight to pack up and go."

Sheba did not reply. She simply left the room.

"Send in Shirley and Shelly," Dunderhead shouted to the royal lackey. "I have something important to tell them."

When Shirley and Shelly arrived, the king informed the girls they would be getting Sheba's land.

"Pa, you're the greatest person who has ever lived. I will be so good to you when you end your career," Shirley intoned.

Shelly, not to be outdone, said, "You are like a god to me, Father. I will be your staff when you put in for the royal pension."

Two years later, on his sixty-fifth birthday, the king announced to the court he would be hanging it up and heading to Miami. "It's been a fabulous fifty years. You've been great subjects. No need to throw me a retirement party. I'll say goodbye to everyone at a farewell lunch next Wednesday in the royal ballroom."

The king had always liked lolling at the beach so he thought Miami a perfect choice for his golden years. But once there he found he was very uncomfortable living in the heat and humidity of south Florida and he missed not experiencing changes of seasons. Dunderhead became depressed and made some bad stock investments. Within six months he was broke.

When the bank began to foreclose the mortgage on his house, the king got on the phone to Shirley. "Darling, I've hit a rough patch and need a place to stay. Can I bunk in with you and your family?"

He was stunned by her reply. "I'm sorry, Dad, but things are crazy here. The kids are screwing up in school, the hubby's work situation is iffy, and the serfs have been slow in paying the rent. I can't possibly take you in. Why don't you give Shelly a buzz?"

When Dunderhead called Shelly, she said, "Unfortunately, I can't put you up right now. The prince and I are going on a round-the-world cruise that departs next Sunday. Try calling Sheba. She's working at a nursing home in Fort Lauderdale. Let me give you her number."

Dunderhead was thunderstruck: *How can my two children, who professed undying admiration for me, be so cruel? How can they treat me so badly?* Dunderhead ruminated on those questions over and over again and he finally became so despondent he was hospitalized.

The king slowly recovered his spirits and one afternoon, during a group therapy session, a group member suggested he call Sheba for assistance. Dunderhead replied he was reluctant to do that because he felt he couldn't face any more family rejection. But other group members said they also thought it would be good idea for the retired ruler to call his daughter. So he did.

"Sheba, I've had some lousy luck and am in a loony bin. I'm better now but I need a place to live. I've asked your sisters for housing but they want nothing to do with me. Can I stay with you?"

Sheba's reply was quick in coming. "Of course you can stay with me, Father. I live in a small one-bedroom condo, but there is a sofa in the living room that opens into a bed and I can sleep on that. The air-conditioning is pretty good in the apartment and I'm a fairly proficient cook. I'm sure you'll enjoy it here. I'll be down in the morning to pick you up."

Dunderhead hung up the phone: *How could I have been such a fool? Why didn't I see it? Shirley and Shelly were shucking me for shekels while Sheba was shoring me up.*

The king recalled that when he was a child he had a tutor who used to tell him, "It's a good idea to 'check the map against the territory'—see if the language a person uses accurately portrays what is going on in the world." Dunderhead had never employed that notion, which he later learned was an important general semantics formulation, but he sure wished he had. He also wished he had followed other GS ideas, such as "look for evidence before making suppositions" and "things can only be known provisionally." However, he decided it's never too late to learn how to do a better job of evaluating things. He would study and become conversant with the formulations of general semantics.

Epilogue

Shirley's husband left her for a younger woman and her children ran away to an orphanage. Shelly and her spouse went down with their cruise ship when it sank in rough seas off the coast of Bermuda. Sheba married a Fortune-500 CEO and she, along with her father, moved to her husband's ten-thousand-acre estate in Palm Beach. Dunderhead obtained an online degree in psychology and went on to become a much sought-after psychotherapist and author of the bestselling book *Your Kids Can Fool You: Useful Advice for Overly-Trusting Parents from a Dad Who Took a Licking but Kept on Ticking.*

Cindy and the Dating Life

It is said, and rightly so, that Cindy Staymore was a creature of habit. She had lived in the same studio apartment for twenty-five years and had the same job and boyfriend for that amount of time. Her clothes were in fashion every decade or so, when the retro look was trending. She made pasta on Mondays, meatloaf on Tuesdays, chicken on Wednesdays, veal on Thursdays, and fish on Fridays. On the weekends Cindy went out for Chinese food or pizza with her beau, Bill Brennan.

They were in a pizzeria when Bill upended her life. "Cindy, I'm getting married to a wonderful girl I really care for. But I want you to know that I've truly enjoyed the time we've spent together. You've been great company."

Cindy finished her pizza and, in a daze, staggered back to her apartment where she screamed into a pillow for six hours, tossed all the food in her cupboards and all the clothes in her closets out the window, and knocked the TV and fish tank over. Then she crawled into bed and fell asleep.

Cindy stayed in bed for a week. She didn't have energy to cook so she ordered out. When the weekend came she felt a bit stronger so on Sunday she took herself to a Chinese restaurant for lunch. At the end of the meal she received a fortune cookie. The message inside it read, "You can't step in the same river twice. Call me if you have a problem with that idea. My number is 1-800-PROCESS."

Cindy put the message in her purse and went back to her apartment. That night she dialed the number contained in the cookie. It belonged to an intellectual soothsayer from Brooklyn. She arranged an appointment with him for the next day.

The oracle turned out to be a bald, heavyset fellow with a Polish accent. He ushered Cindy into his living room and said to her, "What can I do for you?"

Cindy replied, "I didn't understand the message in my fortune cookie. Why can't you step in the same river twice? When I was a child my family and I went on camping trips and we always waded back and forth in the same river."

The seer took out a cigarette, placed it into a long, black cigarette holder; and coolly lit up. Then he said, "The Greek philosopher Heraclitus declared over two thousand years ago that one cannot step in the same river twice because the river is constantly moving. Science has confirmed this process view of existence and has demonstrated that everything in the world is continuously changing—sometimes slowly and sometimes very quickly."

"Well, I don't change," Cindy said. "My life just remains the same."

The fortune-giver replied, "All individuals change over time as new facts present themselves and new circumstances emerge. Are you the same person today that you were a year ago, five years ago, ten years ago? Do you look exactly identical? Has your behavior stayed absolutely the same? It's comforting to think that the world and the people in it are unvarying from day to day; it makes for easy predictability. But life is process, so change must occur."

The sage's words caused Cindy great anxiety. Change might be useful for doing the laundry or buying a newspaper, but the idea that life is process was not a pleasant one to envisage. "I should have gone out for pizza on the weekend," she thought.

The diviner sensed Cindy's discomfort. But he believed it was in her best interest to press forward on the subject of change so he said, "Cindy, have you ever heard of *dating*?"

"Of course I have," Cindy replied. "I dated the same jerk for twenty-five years. I'm an expert on the topic."

"I don't mean that kind of dating. I mean the general-semantics' idea that involves attaching dates to our evaluations to remind us of the fact that we live in a changing world. For example, Iraq (2018) is not Iraq (1998), Joe (who is working out this month) is not Joe (sans workout, last month), and computers (now) are not computers (a decade ago). Dating shows that we live in a restless universe where everything transforms over time."

Cindy wasn't sure about the universe, but *she* was feeling pretty restless. This pudgy prognosticator was making her consider things she had spent her whole life trying to avoid. But she wasn't going to accept reality without a fight.

"Look here! There are times when consistency can be a virtue. We want airline pilots to be consistently alert when they are flying us to our destinations, medicines should have uniform ingredients, and political leaders should stay the course."

The Brooklyn-based prophet responded, "Consistency has nothing to do with it. And, to paraphrase Emerson, consistency is the hobgoblin of little minds. It can keep us from taking risks and expanding our knowledge in new areas. A foolish consistency can hinder us from seeing and making changes that might be beneficial. A hallmark of maturity is to know when to be consistent and when to be flexible."

Cindy had to admit there was more than a modicum of sense in the remarks she was hearing. She had spent her whole life fighting to maintain the status quo but she now saw her battle was doomed from the start. Change was part of the human condition. Change was inevitable. With these verities ringing in her head, Cindy decided tomorrow, Tuesday, would be the first day of the rest of her life. Instead of meatloaf for dinner, she would have sushi.

Amanda and the Good-Looking Plumber

In a major metropolitan region there resided a woman who pined for a plumber. The woman's name was Amanda and the workman she yearned for was Rod. She liked the way he walked, she liked the way he talked, and she liked the way he caulked. But sadly, whenever Rod came to her apartment to do plumbing work, which was fairly often as Amanda constantly broke things in the bathroom and kitchen so Rod could fix them, he barely glanced at her.

"I bet Rod isn't attracted to me because I'm fat," Amanda thought. "A good-looking guy like Rod wants a slim, curvaceous gal."

Now, Amanda wasn't obese or even anything close to it. She was a healthy, bright, thirty-year-old woman whom many would describe as well rounded. Lots of guys found her charming and attractive. But Amanda got it into her head that if she lost thirty-five pounds, Rod would be hers.

Weight loss had never come easy for Amanda but she was determined to get her man. She started on a "no-carb, no-fat, no-sugar, nothing-that-tastes-good diet" and emptied her refrigerator of anything that resembled normal food. She joined a health club where she took power yoga and "Awaken Your Force" classes on alternate evenings. By the end of the first week, Amanda had lost a pound and a half.

"Twenty-four ounces down, five hundred thirty-six to go," she muttered to herself trudging back from the gym to her apartment. "If I keep up with my diet and exercise program I'll hit my goal-weight in a little over twenty-three weeks. Then Rod, that sexy, hot plumber, will be mine."

One Thursday night, after a month of diligent starving and training, Amanda's resolve began to weaken. Instead of going to the health club she felt an urge to stay home to watch TV and eat sweets. Amanda was about to turn on the boob tube and take out a forgotten, frostbitten peach pie from her freezer when an image of Rod, strolling with a beautiful babe on his arm, flashed through her head: *I will not weaken. That chick had better get away from my boyfriend if she knows what's good for her.*

After another month of huffing and puffing and consuming tasteless, nano-sized portions of food, Amanda again felt a desire to stop her Spartan routines. But once again a motivational image came to her, this time in the form of Rod and the aforementioned babe at a fancy ball.

At last, goal-weight day arrived. Amanda stepped on the scale at the health club and the dial hit the magic number. She gazed at herself in the mirror: *No sense being modest. I'm a knockout. I could have any man I want. But I don't want any man. I want Rod.*

That night, Amanda clogged up her toilet with cat litter. She then called Rod to come over to fix the problem. As he worked to clear the toilet, Amanda noticed that he seemed to be talking to her more than he usually did. She took this as a good sign but when she asked Rod to stay for a cup of coffee he said he couldn't and left.

Amanda was perplexed: *Oh, no. I bet he's gay. How could I have been so stupid to have not checked that out!*

Despair often brings people down but sometimes it spurs them to do something smart. That's what it did to Amanda. She remembered she had once dated Rod's business partner Ralph and they had hit it off—platonically. They'd remained friends and had occasionally gone out for drinks. Amanda decided to call Ralph and ask him about Rod.

After some preliminary chitchat, Amanda steered the

conversation to where she wanted it to go.

"Ralph, what's up with Rod? Is he gay?"

Ralph responded with a laugh so hard it caused him to drop his phone. Then he said, "Definitely not! As a matter of fact he had the hots for you. But in the last couple of months he told me his infatuation was waning. He said you were getting skinny."

"Getting skinny? I was thirty-five pounds overweight. Before I went on a drastic diet and exercise regime to lose those pounds, guys barely looked at me when I walked down the street. Now I am constantly getting the once-over from everyone but Rod."

"You poor darling. You should have called me before you embarked on your diet and exercise program. Rod likes his women a bit plump. You were perfect for him when you were heavier."

"How can that be? He barely looked or spoke to me back then."

"That's because Rod is shy around women he is attracted to."

"So the fact that Rod talked to me a lot the last time he saw me is not a sign of romantic interest?"

"It's just the opposite, sweetie."

"Thanks for the information, Ralph. I guess I've made some bad inferences with respect to how Rod perceives members of the opposite sex."

"You sure have. Next time, think like a general semanticist and don't act on inferences as if they were facts. A general semanticist would also tell you that how we label things determines how we react to them. By labeling yourself fat you determined you would be repellent to other people. In doing that you were guilty of libel by label."

Amanda switched off her phone and stared into space for a little while. Then she sat down at her desk, took out a calculator, and added up the number of chicken-nugget, pizza, and hamburger meals she was going to have from the refund of her cancelled health club membership.

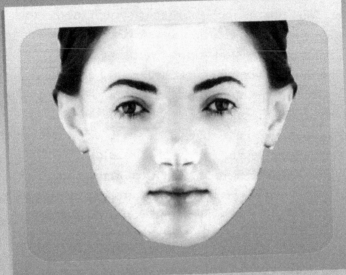

SMARTNESS-1

SMARTNESS-2

SMARTNESS-3

SMARTNESS-4

SMARTNESS-5

SMARTNESS-6

Who's the Smartest One of All

Shane lived in the mundane land of Down-the-Street-From-You—that's a place where Shane lives, but you don't. There he thought he was one smart cookie, and he had every reason to think that. His parents were always saying what an intelligent boy he was and his teachers told him pretty much the same thing. His friends called him "Shane the Brain."

One day, a cousin of his said that there might be some kids around who were smarter than Shane. That remark unsettled him so he went to the school guidance counselor and said, "Mr. Rogers, dean of study hall, who's the smartest one of all?"

The counselor looked over Shane's academic records and replied, "You're definitely the smartest in IQ score, but there are some in other areas who know more."

Shane was furious at this response. "What are you talking about, Mr. Rogers. IQ tests measure how smart someone is or, more precisely, how much smartness someone has. If I score 150 on an IQ test and someone else scores 120, I have more smartness than that person. It's a pretty simple notion."

The counselor smiled, eased back in his chair, and gently said to the livid lad, "It's not as simple as you think, Shane. People don't have smartness. They do smart things and sometimes do stupid things—depending on the circumstances they are in, how much they know about a situation, and how interested in it they are. Smartness is not something you are or have in measurable quantities."

Shane was shocked by these remarks. His parents, teachers, and friends had always told him he was smart. Were they lying to him when they said that? Shane didn't think so.

"Listen, Mr. Rogers, I don't know what you have against me but everyone I know except you thinks I'm smart. I am going to speak to Mrs. Goodenough."

Mrs. Goodenough, a thirty-year veteran of Conventional High and Shane's science teacher, was watering some plants on her desk when Shane entered her office. When she finished that task she looked up at the agitated teen and said, "What can I do for you, my dear?"

Shane's words poured out in a torrent. "Everyone has always told me how smart I am but Mr. Rogers says you can't have smartness. He says you can't even measure it. But that's not true. IQ tests measure smartness and so do grades. Why is Mr. Rogers questioning my intelligence?"

Goodenough chose her words cautiously. "Mr. Rogers is not questioning your intelligence. When people tell you that you're smart they are using that word in a very broad sense. But let's *index* smartness. Indexing is a general semantics technique that, borrowing from mathematics, uses subscript numbers to serve as a reminder that no two things are identical and that examining parts of a larger category can be a valuable way to detect important differences. That said, I am going to label what you do—getting good grades and high scores on IQ tests—as Smartness$_1$. Now come with me and let's see if we can find other kinds of smartness around campus."

They walked to a room where the student council was in session. The council was voting on whether discretionary student funding should go toward having a prom at Chez Moi, the swankiest nightclub in town, or be used to buy books for the school library. The results were 33-4 in favor of the prom.

"The people in this room were elected to their positions so they clearly have superior social skills," Goodenough told Shane. "Let's call the ability to work effectively with others, Smartness$_2$."

Their next stop was the auditorium, which was being used by the school orchestra for a rehearsal. Sammy Pizzicato, a transfer student from Highbrow High, was playing a Mozart violin concerto as they strolled in.

"Sammy sounds good," Mrs. Goodenough said. "Maybe this year our orchestra can finish in a position higher than last in the annual city-wide high school orchestra contest. Anyway, let's designate Sammy's ability to play the violin, Smartness$_3$."

The counselor and her charge moseyed over to the gym. There they saw Jock Johnson, a 6'7" senior who had an allergy to reading books and anything else containing words, effortlessly dunking basketballs. "Jock may not be the brightest bulb on the Christmas tree with respect to academic skills," Mrs. Goodenough opined, "but our basketball coach tells me he shines in sports. Twelve colleges have offered him athletic scholarships. Let's classify Jock's ability to move deftly around the basketball court, Smartness$_4$."

They proceeded to the school library. On the librarian's desk was the latest copy of *The Conformist*, the literary journal of Conventional High. Goodenough picked it up and said to Shane, "This issue contains three poems by your classmate, Willie Wordsworth. My favorite of them is 'Cellphone Free: The Only Way To Be,' but I also like 'My Dad Is Working Himself to Death so My Family Can Have Lots of Junk.' Willie seems to have a real capacity to understand himself. Let's categorize that ability, Smartness$_5$."

When they got back to Goodenough's office, the teacher said to Shane, "Are you smart in all the areas we have just seen? Probably not. But that doesn't take away any of your worth as a human being. I'm sure you're smart enough to realize that."

Shane wasn't so sure. He had thought himself special, a genius perhaps, but now he figured being intellectually gifted was only one form of smartness. That revelation was not going to be easy to live with.

"Mrs. Goodenough," Shane said in a quivering voice, "my whole identity has been wrapped up in being smart. Now I see that I'm only partly smart. There are others in different domains who are smarter than me. I feel like I've gone from being 'Shane the Brain' to 'Plain

Shane.' I'm sorry I came to school today. I should have stayed home."

Goodenough was not about to let Shane succumb to self-pity. "Shane, you're talking nonsense and you're making things worse with that 'Plain Shane' business. It's not a good idea to rate yourself. Try to be self-accepting or, if you must, rate your characteristics. For example, 'I'm okay at tennis,' 'lousy at cooking,' 'good at taking tests,' and so on. That would be a smart thing to do."

Shane considered Goodenough's words. Being okay at tennis or good at taking tests was not the same as being Shane the Brain but somehow it felt closer to reality. "You know what, Mrs. Goodenough. I think I'll take your advice. I will focus on stuff I'm interested in and stop characterizing myself as smart or special or plain or using some other broad term."

"Good idea, Shane. You'll get more accomplished that way and have more fun doing things."

"Thanks for all your help, Mrs. Goodenough. I'm going to pop in on Mr. Rogers for a few minutes. Catch you later."

Rogers was busy doing paperwork when Shane knocked on his door. He got up to open it.

"A pleasure to see you, Shane. I hope you had a nice talk with Mrs. Goodenough."

"I did, Mr. Rogers. I also took a nice trip with her around the campus. It was most enlightening."

"That's great, Shane. I'm a big fan of enlightenment. You know that word signifies an eighteenth-century philosophical movement that focused on criticizing previously accepted doctrines through rational thought."

"I do know that. We studied the Enlightenment in history last year. Our country is a product of its thinking. Mr. Rogers, I'd like to finish this story in rhyme. Would you care to accompany me in a lyrical dialogue?"

The counselor grinned and replied, "If you got the time, I got the rhyme."

Coda

Shane: "My favorite dean of study hall, do you think I can get into Harvard in the fall?"

Rogers: "High grades can help you to attain that goal, and it sure wouldn't hurt to make the honor roll."

Shane: "I'll study hard, Mr. Rogers, and do my best, to gain lots of knowledge and ace my tests."

Rogers: "That would be a tremendously smart thing to do, and you might also want to audition for the band and crew."

Shane: "That's a great suggestion; you've earned my gratitude and praise. I now think about smartness in multiple ways."

The Wisdom of Delay

King Crouton carefully looked over the three young men who stood before him. They were handsome and talented princes with noble lineage and in less than a fortnight he would be selecting one of them to marry his daughter. The question the king was wrestling with was which one to choose.

Melvin the Magician, Merlin's younger brother, had suggested that Crouton set a test for the princes and the one who did best on it would get the girl. The king thought Melvin's idea was a clever solution to his problem. But what examination should he give the princes? Melvin, again, came up with an answer.

"Your Highness, like any caring father I am sure you want your daughter to wed a fellow with good judgment. Why don't you place these guys in situations where that quality can be examined?"

Princes' Alf, Bart, and Chuck were shifting nervously on their feet as Crouton addressed them. "Gentlemen, I have devised a test to help me figure out which one of you should marry Princess Matilda. It's a three-part exam. Part one involves slaying the three-headed dragon that lives in the Valley of Despair. I give you two days to complete the task. Good luck and good hunting."

The princes set out at once on their dragon-killing quest. Alf was the first to encounter trouble. There was a long line of riders and coaches at the toll leading to the Valley of Despair and he did not have his EZ Pass or exact change to speed him through, unlike Bart and

Chuck who whizzed by him with EZ Passes on their saddles.

"Those jokers will get to the dragon before me and I won't have a chance to slay the beast," Alf thought. "I better take my steed out of the cash line and jump over the tollgate." Alas, that was a bad decision. Alf was pulled over by a toll enforcement officer and placed under arrest. His impatience had cost him the opportunity to kill the dragon.

Bart and Chuck arrived at the Valley late at night. Since he had been travelling all day, Chuck, who was a student of general semantics and so was in the habit of delaying his reactions and thinking things through, decided he would rest and look for the dragon in the morning. Bart, who liked to react to things quickly—in the jargon of general semantics he exhibited "signal reactions"—had other plans. He lit his trusty torch and went into the woods to seek the creature.

At daybreak, Chuck awoke and discovered he was but a few feet from the dragon's lair, where the mythical beast was sleeping and snoring loudly through its six nostrils. With three quick strokes Chuck chopped the monster's heads off and put them in a sack. Then he got on his horse and started back to Crouton's castle. On the way he noticed Bart, still in slumber, alongside the road.

When he reached the castle, the king congratulated Chuck for his dragon-slaying success. Two days later he laid out the second part of the test to the three princes. Alf, released on bail, was particularly attentive as Crouton spoke. "Get me Excalibur, the legendary sword of King Arthur, which is impaled in a rock in the middle of Lake Caesar Salad. You have four days to do it, boys."

The three princes mounted their charges and rode for the lake. When they got there they could see Excalibur's exquisite jeweled handle and gleaming bright blade sticking out of a large jagged rock a few hundred feet from the shore.

"I'm going in," Alf shouted. And in he went, but not too far, for Alf had never learned to swim and though Lake Caesar Salad is only two-feet deep at the shoreline, it quickly drops to a depth of well over five-hundred feet. Fortunately, Bart and Chuck were able to save poor Alf from becoming food for fish.

Bart was determined to beat Chuck to the sword, so after dragging

Alf from the water he dove back into the lake and headed for Excalibur. The problem was, once he got to the sword he couldn't pull it out. Bart got so tired from trying to free the sword that he barely made it back to dry land.

Chuck had paid attention on the day that Arthurian legends were being taught in his high school English class so he knew that only the rightful king of Britain would be able to remove Excalibur from the rock. As he was not sure he was that king, he decided to hire a boat and row to the rock that held Excalibur, put the rock in the boat, return to the shore, put the whole caboodle in a wagon, and convey the contents to the king.

After congratulating Chuck on his second victory, Crouton spelled out the last part of the test to the princes: "Bring me the pot of gold that sits at the end of the rainbow. I'll give you a week to accomplish this."

Alf and Bart were feeling desperate. They were losing to Chuck two to nothing and knew if they didn't make a big success in this final contest they could kiss off any dream of having the king as an in-law and the lovely Matilda as a wife. They asked the royal meteorologist for his three-day weather forecast. The weatherman replied, "It looks like two days of sun and then, maybe, on day three a slight chance of showers." Alf and Bart dashed off to the royal chapel to pray for rain.

Chuck mused on the matter: *The king was fairly straightforward in his last two requests. I wonder if now he is being a bit tricky. Let me think on this.*

Bingo! Chuck recalled that the Rainbow Bar and Grill was located next to the First Royal Bank. That financial institution was holding a promotion: open a five-thousand-dollar savings account, get a gold-plated pot.

Chuck phoned his father and asked him for a loan of five Gs, which he promised to pay back with interest. His dad agreed to the request and Chuck took the borrowed dough to the First Royal Bank where he opened a savings account and was presented with a gold-plated pot that he proudly delivered to King Crouton.

"Prince Chuck, in the tests I gave, you delayed your reactions long enough to investigate and respond to circumstances in a thoughtful manner. This brought you success in your efforts and it will bring you Matilda for a wife. Welcome to the family, Chucky boy."

Chucky boy? I don't want to be called "Chucky boy." What if I called you "breadcrumb boy?" What if I said I'm glad you're past your salad days? I'd bet you'd think those were dumb remarks. Chuck wanted to say those words to King Crouton but he didn't because he made it a practice to delay his reactions and think about things. There would be time after the wedding to deal with his father-in-law's intemperate comments. And someday he would be ruler of the kingdom. So Chuck responded, "I look forward to marrying your beautiful daughter and being part of your illustrious clan. I toast your good health. May you 'flour' in all that you do."

Einstein and Elmer the Elementalist

I n a time before now, but not before then, there lived a suggestible fellow named Elmer who had, in the idiom of general semantics, *elementalistic tendencies*. Such leanings involve the use of words to seek *the* cause of something—e.g., *the* cause of juvenile delinquency, *the* cure for cancer, *the* way to raise children—unconsciously assuming there is only one cause. "What's wrong with that?" you say. Let's look at some things that happened to Elmer and see.

As a youth Elmer was told by his father, "*The* way to get ahead in business is to work hard and play by the rules." Since his old man was the CEO of a major global corporation, Elmer figured his dad knew what he was talking about.

When Elmer got his first job he used his father's advice as *the* way to get ahead at work. Unfortunately, Elmer's quest to move up the organizational ladder in his company was continuously stymied because the road to advancement there was through office politics and being pushy. It was only when he revised his father's model, to take into account the realities of the place where he was actually working, that he began to stop crying himself to sleep at night over his frustration at being thwarted in his career and started to have some hope for advancement.

On the romantic front, Elmer took his courtship cues from what his mother had told him when he was thirteen. She had said, "*The* way to win a girl's heart is to treat her like a queen and cater to her every wish. That's what your father did in wooing me and it worked. I couldn't wait to marry him."

Elmer used his mother's guidance in courting girls, which won him the affection of many of the women he went out with. But it did not gain him the love of Sarah Standoffish, the woman he really desired. When she broke off their relationship Sarah told him, "You're a nice guy, Elmer, but you're too much of a doormat. I don't want to be with a 'yes-man.' I want a guy who will stand up to me when I make outrageous demands."

In health matters, Elmer believed that the mind and the body were not connected and that *the* cause of physical illness was physical. So it puzzled him when his internist suggested he see a psychiatrist to help alleviate his recurring ulcer attacks. The doctor said, "People talk about *the* 'mind' and *the* 'body' as if they were separate from each other. But that's not correct. Chemical processes of the body affect the mind— that's why antidepressants work. And the opposite is true. Our mental state can influence our physical condition—worry can aggravate ulcers and other bodily ailments. We would all be better off considering 'mind/body' as a process rather than mind and body as discrete entities."

When Elmer left the doctor's office he headed for his favorite place in the world to think—Bernie's Bar. When he got there he ordered a scotch and milk and a bag of peanuts. On a barstool next to him was a bushy-headed man who looked just like Albert Einstein. The fellow was imbibing a German Riesling and telling the bartender that it was an excellent choice for people who preferred wine with low alcoholic content.

"Excuse me," Elmer said to his Riesling-drinking neighbor, "has anyone ever told you that you look like Albert Einstein?"

"I have been told that many times. And well I should for I am Albert Einstein."

"Are you kidding?" Elmer gasped. "What do you mean you're Albert Einstein?"

"I mean I am Albert Einstein," the fluffy-haired fellow said. "When I died, in nineteen fifty-five, I went to the great beyond where I worked at refining my time and space equations. As a result of those efforts I came up with a formula for time travel. I now go back and forth between heaven and earth, quite often actually. I particularly enjoy coming to Bernie's for the Riesling and the sawdust on the floor. It's hard to find sawdust in bars today."

"That's an amazing story!" Elmer said in a resonant and respectful tone. "It really is."

"Bernie's peanuts are also amazing," Einstein replied. "I see you ordered a bag, too."

"Yes, I did. And I'm going to order another scotch and milk. I've had a tough day. My doctor told me to see a psychiatrist. Apparently, what you think can affect you physically."

"That's true," Einstein responded. "The 'mind' and the 'body' are not detached from each other. Can there be a mind without a body? Lacking a body, there would be no mind. And without the mind, what would the body be? Mind and body are interrelated."

"That's also what my doctor said. Can I ask you a question, Mr. Einstein?"

"Sure, as long as it's not 'What's it like in heaven?' The guy who lets me live up there has told me I'm not supposed to answer that one. And call me Al. Mr. Einstein was my father."

"Okay, Al. Here's the deal. I've always looked for *the* way to do this or *the* way to do that or *the* cause for this or *the* cause for that. But I've had some experiences lately that have led me to question the wisdom of thinking in such a manner. I'd like to ask you, 'What's the best way to think about things?'"

"That's too broad a question for me to answer," Einstein replied. "You constrain your possibilities to come up with a good solution if you say *the* way to do this or *the* way to do that. There is usually more than just one way to do something. And here's another piece of advice: people often miss the big picture in situations because they use isolated words to define them. If I had done that I would not have come up with the notion of 'space-time' in my mathematical formulas. Connecting certain terms that are split through language, like 'space' and 'time,' but are linked in the natural world, makes sense. General semanticists suggest hyphenating those terms. For example, 'psycho-somatic,' 'socio-cultural,' and 'neuro-linguistic.'"

"That's helpful, Al, but I don't like using hyphens. My dislike of them stems from when I was a kid in the fifth grade and my teacher put the heading 'stupid-dumb-idiots' on the blackboard. If a student did anything wrong their name would be listed under that banner. I did lots of things wrong so my name appeared many times as a stupid-dumb-idiot, which turned me off to hyphenated language. Is there another way to grasp the interrelatedness of particular words?"

"Try this formulation from general semantics: place quotes around words that involve related ideas. For example, thoughts influence feelings and feelings influence thoughts. So when you're talking about 'thoughts' and 'feelings' put quotes around them in your mind. That will help you to be sensitive to their interdependence."

"That's a super suggestion, Al. How about giving me some additional thinking tips."

"Sorry, no can do. I have an appointment in ten minutes with my landlord in paradise and if I don't show up on time there'll be hell to pay. But I'll be back here next Tuesday."

"Well, it was nice to have met you, Al. And I look forward to seeing you next week. Will you be coming by at any special hour?"

"I usually drop in around eight in the evening. That's when the karaoke singing begins. I do a mean rendition of 'Time after Time,' and my 'Travellin' Man' is always a huge hit with the crowd. After the singing, Bernie sells t-shirts that have my picture on the front with a message that reads, "When it comes to physics, Einstein's *the* man." Because I thought that caption was elementalistic, on the back of the shirts I had Bernie add images of Galileo and Newton with words that say, "And don't forget about these two guys."

A Know-It-All's Transformation

In a world where people are often late for appointments, irregular in their ablutions, and sometimes tardy in paying the rent, Wally Wiseapple was a model of virtue. He was punctual in his engagements, he bathed every day, and he mailed his lodging remittances before the tenth of each month. Alas, Wally had one significant fault. He was a know-it-all. Ask him a question about the Middle East and Wally would reply, "Let me tell you all about the Middle East." If the topic swung around to religion, you could count on Wally to declare, "I know everything about spiritual matters." When sports were being discussed, Wally was wont to say, "There's nothing anyone can teach me about athletics." Whatever the subject, Wally knew all about it.

Now the fact is, no one can know *all* about anything. And while this statement may seem obvious to you, it certainly wasn't to Wally. He thought he knew what it is impossible to know: everything about everything.

One day, Wally received a call from the producers of the TV program *Jeopardy*: "Wally, we've reviewed your audition tape and we want you as a contestant. Please come down to the studio tomorrow afternoon to be on the show."

Wally was pretty calm when the cameras began to roll. He figured he'd beat his opponents easily since he knew all that there was to know: *How much could they know? Undoubtedly, less than me.*

Wally did well in the first Jeopardy round. He did even better in round number two. When the final Jeopardy question was announced, Wally had a substantial money lead over his two competitors. The final question was "Who was the only president to have remained a bachelor throughout his life?" Wally wrote down James Monroe. The correct answer was James Buchanan.

Since Wally had wagered all his money on the final question he was left with nothing when he got the question wrong. His two rivals came up with the right response. Wally finished last.

Wally was teased quite a bit at work the next day: "I guess Mr. Know-It-All doesn't know all that much." "How could a bright guy like you not know stuff about American presidents?" "Well, you got half the question right. The president's first name was James."

Wally felt hurt by these remarks and his self-confidence started to slip. He began to isolate himself from others because he didn't want to take a chance on saying something that was wrong.

One afternoon, when Wally was moping in the employees' cafeteria, Peggy Pleasant, an affable administrative assistant from the HR department, sat down next to him.

"How's it going, Wally?"

"So-so," he replied. "How are things with you, Peggy?"

"Things are good. I'm getting a raise."

"That's nice. You're a hard worker. You deserve it."

"Thanks for the compliment, Wally. I believe a course I'm taking on how to improve your thinking through the formulations of general semantics helped me get the extra money. Maybe you should take that course too."

"Why? Do you think I'm a lousy thinker?"

"I think we can all use help in improving our thinking skills. Anyway, if you're interested, the course meets Wednesday nights at seven at the high school on Main Street. The topic this week is how to surmount *allness attitudes.*"

When Wally went home that night he thought about his conversation with Peggy and concluded he'd have little to lose if he took a course on enhancing one's thinking ability. And he was curious what the teacher would say about allness attitudes.

Peggy waved to Wally when he entered the high school classroom. He was late and the instructor was already speaking.

"People who think they know all about things are demonstrating allness attitudes. Such attitudes are quite common and relatively easy to spot in others but detecting them in ourselves is a harder proposition. More difficult still is coming up with ideas to keep us flexible and away from allness thinking."

"You got that right," Wally muttered to himself as the teacher continued his presentation.

"Science tells us that we can't know all about the world or anything in it. Therefore, our mental maps of reality are always incomplete. Accepting this idea allows us to be more open to acquiring new information on various topics."

Wally thought that proposition had some merit and that gaining new information about things might not be such a bad thing to do.

"Another good way to defeat allness inclinations is to employ terms like 'to me,' 'I think,' and 'it seems,' when making statements. Such expressions make it clear that our observations and opinions have definite limits. For example, '*To me*, pizza is the most delicious food in the world.' '*I think* New York City is the best place to live.' '*It seems* likely it will snow today.'"

The concept of using qualifying terms in conversations made a lot of sense to Wally and he resolved to try it out.

"Lastly," the instructor concluded, "one can add a silent 'etcetera' to one's thinking as a reminder that there is always more that can be learned, more that can be said."

Wally decided he would add more than one etcetera to his thinking: *Given my penchant for making allness statements, I think I'll be like Yul Brynner in* The King and I. *When it comes to etcetera, I'll add three.*

Wally assiduously applied his newfound knowledge on how to overcome allness attitudes and found it greatly improved his ability to reason clearly and get along better with others. Over the next year he was promoted several times at work and was designated employee of the month for three months running. Wally was also elected president of the local chapter of the International Listening Association and he married Peggy Pleasant.

To some of his colleagues, Wally's success and good fortune in turning his life around seemed like something out of a fairy tale. But what happened to Wally is well within the realm of possibility. More bizarre things have certainly occurred in real life. For example, heroin was once a perfectly acceptable medicine prescribed by doctors as a cough suppressant. And just as incredible (maybe even more so), prior to the 1960s tobacco companies ran physician-endorsed ads that suggested smoking had health benefits. One would be hard-pressed to find a story crazier than that.

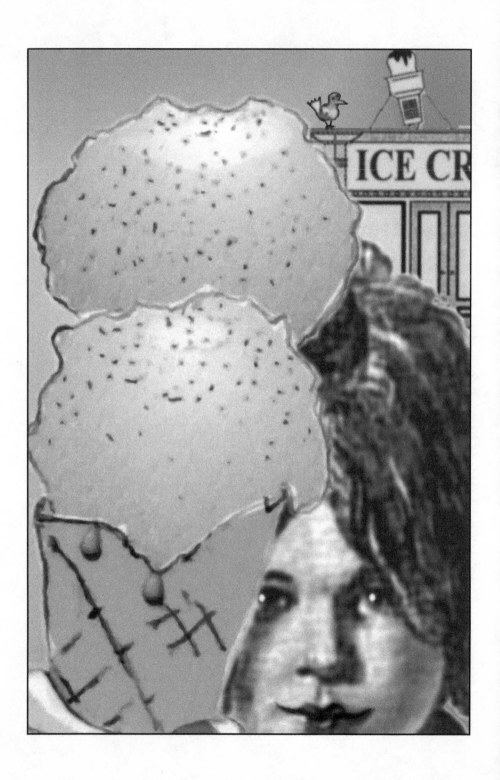

Frieda and the IFD Disease

Frieda Fischer was a fortunate frau who had what most people would consider a fabulous life, to wit: a loving husband, two healthy well-behaved children, a six-bedroom house with a white picket fence, a seven-figure savings account balance, freedom to work as a lawyer or be a stay-at-home mom, a Springer spaniel named Spencer, a Jaguar Convertible, and Wednesday nights out with the girls. Frieda also had medical insurance that covered outpatient mental health care, which she took liberal advantage of.

In therapy, Frieda discussed a problem that had plagued her all her life—an inability to find "true" happiness and success. Various therapists had tried to help her solve that problem but their efforts had proven futile. She was on the verge of checking herself into a very expensive psychiatric hospital when she spied a small advertisement in a local newspaper. It read, "True happiness and success exist only in fairy tales. For information on attaining real-life satisfactions contact Dr. Pragmato." Frieda called the number listed in the ad and made an appointment to see the doctor.

When Frieda entered Pragmato's office he was on the phone. When he finished his conversation he looked up at her and said, "How may I help you?"

"I feel great frustration at not being truly happy and successful," Frieda said, "and I've become quite depressed about the matter."

"What is your definition of true happiness and success?" the doctor asked.

"People who are truly happy and successful can do exactly what they want and they never fail at anything."

"Do you know anyone who fits that description?"

"No, not personally. But I'm sure there are people like that around."

Pragmato leaned back in his chair and stroked his goatee, a style of facial hair that has been worn through the ages by all sorts of people including famous ones such as Cardinal Richelieu, Charles Dickens, and Tupac Shakur. Then he said, "I think you are suffering from *IFD disease.*"

"What the heck is that?" Frieda replied.

"IFD disease is a term coined by Wendell Johnson in his book *People in Quandaries: The Semantics of Personal Adjustment.*[1] It describes a condition in which frustration in achieving high ideals can lead a person to become discouraged. IFD specifically refers to an individual going from a state of **I**dealization to **F**rustration to **D**emoralization. It's a form of craziness in that glorified goals, such as true happiness and success, are vague standards that have no objective referents in the 'real world.'"

"Craziness? Do you think I'm crazy, doctor?"

"Of course not. You're a highly functional young woman who is dealing really well with many important responsibilities. You are definitely not crazy. You are simply thinking in a less than sane manner with respect to your notions of true happiness and success."

"Can I learn to think more sanely about those things?"

"I believe you can and to do that I suggest studying general semantics, a science-based 'self-help' system designed to assist individuals to better evaluate and overcome everyday difficulties. General semantics is described in *People in Quandaries*, the book I alluded to earlier."

"Will that book also teach me how to get over IFD disease?"

---

[1] Wendell Johnson, *People in Quandaries: The Semantics of Personal Adjustment* (Concord, CA: International Society for General Semantics, 2002).

"It will, Frieda, and so will I. The trick to getting over IFD disease is to use *operational definitions* for vague ideas like "happiness" and "success." For example, happiness is having the baseball team you root for win the World Series; success is figuring out *The New York Times* crossword puzzle. If it is not these things, then happiness or success must be something you *do* or can imagine yourself doing, something specific and achievable."

"Well, I have engaged in and achieved a number of things in my life. I did well in college and grad school, I have a great career, a terrific husband, two delightful children, fine friends, good health and, if you can stand the compliment doctor, a wonderful shrink."

"Thanks for the props, Frieda. I'm pleased when patients praise my work. But more to the point, I hope I have convinced you to renounce your search for 'true' happiness and success. They are verbal illusions. Instead of pursuing such fantasies just do what you think is worthwhile doing. If you don't succeed at a particular thing, console yourself with G.K. Chesterton's words, "If a thing is worth doing, it is worth doing badly."

"That's a great quote, doc. When I get home I am going to type it out on the computer and frame it. I must say, this has been a very productive visit for me."

"I'm glad to hear that, Frieda. If you work on what I've told you I think you will feel much better."

"You know what would make me feel better right now, Doctor Pragmato?"

"I have no idea, Frieda."

"Having a double scoop of Baskin-Robbins' Very Berry Strawberry ice cream topped with rainbow sprinkles, marshmallows, and peanuts on a fresh-baked waffle cone."

"You're in luck! There's a Baskin-Robbins ice cream parlor down the block. I suggest you go over there right now and chill out. As a matter of fact, I think I'll join you."

Sam and the Strange Bird

In the hallowed hills of Beverly, an affluent realm on America's West Coast, there dwelled an outstanding student with the commonplace appellation, Sam. The lad never got less than ninety-five in a major subject nor less than ninety-eight in a minor one. He excelled at sports, debate, and playing the oboe. With a winning smile and sweet disposition, you would have thought Sam would be feeling like the king of the hill. You would have been wrong.

Sam believed it was horrible to be ignored at any point during a conversation. This belief caused him great unhappiness because he felt hurt every time he talked to someone and they did not pay attention to everything he said. Sam managed to conceal his pain in elementary and middle school but his suffering got so bad in junior high school that he decided to bump himself off.

Sam stepped onto the ledge outside his ninth-floor bedroom window and was about to jump when a small yellow bird with a 150 IQ and the ability to talk, landed next to him.

"What's up, dude?"

"Oh my gosh, you can speak!"

"That's true, and I can fly. But you can't. What are you doing out here?"

Sam explained his plight to the bird. When he finished, the flying creature said, "I agree that it's no fun to gab with others and have them ignore you. I've had that experience myself. I'll be twittering happily along and one of my fine-feathered friends, or maybe the whole flock, will tune me out. I hate when that happens."

"How can the other birds understand you? Do they speak English?"

"Of course not," the bird said. "They're a bunch of birdbrains. Fortunately, I'm bilingual. In addition to English, I speak 'chirp-and-cheep.'"

Sam was amazed that he was having an intelligent discussion with a bird, and a rather polite one at that. The little yellow fellow had not ignored him once during their colloquy.

"Don't you feel terrible when you are being dissed by the other birds? Don't you think there must be something wrong with you?"

"Not really," the bird responded. "I don't think I'm so spellbinding that I can continuously hold the attention of every winged beast I speak with. Of course, if I truly want attention I talk to people. They seem fascinated by whatever I say."

"I can understand that," Sam replied. "And you pronounce your words so clearly."

"I believe it's not just what you say, but how you say it. The news anchors on network TV, with their Midwest inflections, are my role models for proper enunciation."

"Well, you are certainly a masterful speaker and I've enjoyed talking with you," Sam said, "but life has become unbearable for me. I think I'll take the plunge."

"Hold your horses, young man. Before you do a swan dive, let me give your situation some thought. Maybe I can come up with a substitute plan for you."

"Okay. I'll give you two minutes to think of something."

"I got it!" the bird tweeted. "May I ask you a question?"

"Sure," Sam replied.

"Do you think you are being ignored in conversations more than other people?"

"I don't know," said Sam. "It feels like I am, but to be honest with you I've never thought about other people being ignored in conversations. I guess I've been too busy thinking about me rather than observing what's happening with others."

"Well, I think it's important to know if you're being singled out for special treatment in discussions and I have an approach you can use to find that out."

"What's the approach?"

"It's called the *scientific method*. I learned about its value in solving everyday problems in a general semantics course I took with a gaggle of geese at Golden State University a few years ago.

Sam had learned about the scientific method in middle school. As he recalled, its main tenets were *observe, test, evaluate.* He had used that formula in his science-lab experiments.

"I know the scientific method works in the laboratory, but can it help to solve personal problems in real life?" Sam asked.

"Absolutely," the airborne vertebrate responded. "I've used the scientific method many times to handle difficulties and have gotten excellent results. I employed it a couple of weeks ago to help me get over my fear of rejection in asking chicks out for a date. I conducted an experiment where I invited one-hundred different female birds who I met while flying over Griffith Park to have dinner with me."

"How did that work out?"

"Well, only two of the gals accepted my invitation, and they never showed up at the pond that I booked for our rendezvous. But I totally got over my fear of rejection."

"Okay," said Sam, "I'll give the scientific method a try. What do I have to do?"

"I want you to conduct a two-part test. For the first part you will need to observe student conversations in the school cafeteria for two weeks to determine the extent to which people ignore each other when talking. I'll meet you back on the ledge in a fortnight to discuss your findings."

Sam followed his avian mentor's instructions and in so doing witnessed numerous instances of students ignoring each other during verbal exchanges. He concluded such behavior was not unusual. It was actually ordinary.

The bird listened with rapt attention when Sam reported the results of his research. "You've done a great job, my friend. I now want you to interview twenty-five randomly selected students to learn their views about being ignored during conversations. Can you do that?"

"I'm on the case!" Sam replied.

The responses Sam received in his interviews were varied but basically fell into three categories: "Being ignored in conversations doesn't bother me at all." "I can't stand being ignored." "Since you can't control other people's reactions it doesn't pay to get overly upset about being ignored."

The last response was by far the most popular and, combined with his observations of student discussions in the school cafeteria, helped Sam to understand that one does not have to become a hermit or suicidal if one is not listened to with complete attention during all parts of a conversation. And, while this may not seem like much of an insight to most people, it certainly was to Sam, who had a strange bird and the scientific method to thank for it.

The Wizard of "Is"

This is the story of Betty the Blowhard, a blustering woman who was not an easy person to talk to. You think I'm exaggerating that conversations with Betty were tough? Consider the following discussion between Betty and her coworker, Bonnie.

Bonnie: I saw *The Godfather* at a revival film festival yesterday. I really enjoyed it.

Betty: That was the best movie ever made. Nothing comes close to it.

Bonnie: I've liked other movies equally well. I found *Citizen Kane* and *Lawrence of Arabia* quite entertaining.

Betty: They don't hold a candle to *The Godfather*. Francis Ford Coppola is the best director who ever lived and nobody acts better than Brando and Pacino. You obviously don't know much about movies.

Bonnie: Maybe not, but I know what I like. Anyway, after the movie I went to the Museum of Modern Art and caught their latest exhibit. I thought it was very interesting.

Betty: Modern art isn't art. It's hype and pretense disguised as art. There's no real art anymore. Art went out in the nineteenth century.

Bonnie: You're entitled to your opinion, Betty, but I disagree. I think modern art is in every sense art. Let's talk about something else.

Betty: Okay. Did I tell you that I went out to dinner at Chez Magnifique last night? *The New York Times* gave that restaurant four stars even though *it's* got the worst food in the city. No one could like that food. I'm surprised the restaurant is still in business.

Bonnie: Whatever you say, Betty. Listen, I can't talk anymore. I've to get back to work.

Weekends were tough for Betty. Her dogmatic conversational style caused her to have no friends and her parents didn't want her over for visits. Though she occasionally dated (Betty was physically attractive and knew lots of things about all sorts of stuff), her relationships never lasted long. Betty's two main companions were her cat and her television.

Dr. Friedrich Flugelman, Betty's therapist, had persistently tried to get Betty to understand that her unequivocal positions turned people off. But he had been unsuccessful in helping her to see this. "Dr. Flugelman," Betty said, "I tell it like it is."

One day, Betty told Flugelman that he was the worst psychologist in the world. He responded by saying, "Betty, I have worked with you for five years and we haven't made much progress. I think you should see someone else."

Betty went home that night and spoke to her cat. "Schrodinger, you're the only one I can really communicate with. That's not a good situation for a twenty-nine-year-old woman who wants to get hitched and have children. I so want things to change for me. I truly do."

At that moment her doorbell rang. It was Frank Wizard, a neighbor from the apartment across the hall. "Sorry to bother you, Betty," he said, "but could I borrow a cup of sugar? My mom is coming to visit me and I want to bake her a cake."

Betty liked Frank. He was tall, tanned, and sported nifty tattoos on his biceps that read, "I love Mom." He was also a gentleman. Frank always held the door open for Betty in the building lobby.

"Is it only sugar you need, Frank? I also have butter, eggs, flour, a Williams-Sonoma rolling pin, a cutting board, a mixer, and a wide assortment of all-purpose baking pans."

"Thanks, Betty. I think the sugar will do just fine."

"Okay. By the way, what kind of cake are you making?"

"Devil's food cake."

"That's not a great cake to make, Frank. It's too chocolaty."

"For my mother, there is no such thing as something being too chocolaty. She's a big a fan of chocolate."

"Suit yourself. I was only trying to be helpful."

"Thanks, Betty. I always like hearing your opinions."

"I wasn't giving you my opinion, Frank. Devil's food cake *does* contain too much chocolate."

Frank didn't immediately respond to this remark because he did not want to get into an argument with his neighbor. But he did want to make a comment on it so he said, "Betty, when you say devil's food cake contains too much chocolate you're telling me very little about what you are describing. You are telling me instead, something about yourself. You are projecting your idea of what you consider to be too much chocolate. You are confusing opinions with facts."

Betty's positive feelings for Frank overrode her desire to debate so she said, "That's interesting. What do you suggest I do about my confusion?"

"I suggest you use qualifying expressions like 'it seems to me,' or 'as I see it,' or 'from my point of view' when you talk about things like devil's food cake having too much chocolate in it. Such phrases signal to others that you are communicating your beliefs, not absolute truths."

"Well, Frank, it seems to me that you know something about human communication. Are you a therapist?"

"No, I'm a welder. But what I do is a little like therapy. I repair damaged connections."

Betty liked the metaphor. She also liked the metaphor-maker so she decided to level with him. "Frank, I've been told by lots of people that I have a problem separating what is going on in the world around me from what I say about it. Do you think you can help me to overcome that difficulty?"

"I think I can, Betty. I'm a student of general semantics and I've learned from that discipline that the word 'is' can contribute to the problem you described. When a person uses 'is' to link a noun and an adjective modifying that noun he or she may unconsciously project. For example, when we say 'He is lazy,' or 'She is smart,' we are suggesting that 'laziness' is found in him or that 'smartness' is found in her. This contradicts what is really going on: we are projecting our *opinions* concerning 'laziness' and 'smartness' onto other people. Qualifying our responses conveys that reality—for example, 'He seems lazy to me,' or 'From my point of view she is smart.'"

Betty's initial thought on what Frank had just told her was "Frank is the smartest guy in the world" and "Frank is simply perfect." However she now knew that thinking this way was factually incorrect: *To be more accurate I should describe Frank as being perfect to me or say, from my vantage point Frank is the smartest man in the world.* While she understood that reasoning in this manner would not be easy to do, Betty decided to give it a try.

It took some time, but through persistence and hard work Betty overcame her propensity for pomposity and when he proposed she married Frank. They moved to a house in the suburbs where they live today with a dog, a cat, and two junior Wizards. Frank manages his own construction company and Betty, through her study of general semantics, has become a highly successful communications consultant. It's a fool's bet to prophesy that Frank and Betty will live happily ever after but for the nonce, they both seem pretty happy to me.

The Tale of the Greedy Wisher

"I thought you get three wishes for saving a genie in a bottle."

"That's normally true, Fred," the genie replied, "and believe me, if I could give you three wishes, or three hundred wishes, I would. Unfortunately genie power, like other forms of energy, has been vastly depleted over the last decade. I'm afraid I can offer you only one wish. Try to make it a good one."

Fred thought the genie was probably telling the truth. Why would he lie and risk being thrown back into the ocean? But Fred was determined to get more than one wish so he said, "I'll agree to be given only one wish, but you have to promise that whatever it is, you'll fulfill it."

"Of course, master. Granting wishes is what we genies do for a living. We're the experts in the wish fulfillment business. Please make your wish known."

"My wish is for you to grant me as many requests as I make of you. That means if I say I want this, I get it. And if I say I want that, I get it too. That's my wish."

"Fred, you are asking for something that would be wrong for me to do. If I go along with your desire I will reduce the energy supply of genies everywhere. People, especially children, will not have the things they wish for come to pass. I'm sure you wouldn't want that to happen."

"How do you know what I want? Look, genie, I don't think you're in a particularly good position to negotiate. So what's it going to be? Will you consent to do my bidding or do I fling you back into the sea?"

The genie, severely cramped by the glass that encircled him, responded meekly, "All right, I guess I'm stuck. I accept your demand that I furnish anything you ask of me. Now will you please let me out of here."

Fred uncorked the bottle and the genie swooshed up into the heavens. "Wow! It's awesome to be free and in the open air. Don't leave. I'm going to do a quick lap around the planet. Be back in a minute." And with that the genie disappeared over the horizon.

Sixty seconds later, the genie reappeared. "I can't believe how good I feel. I haven't worked out in nine hundred years yet I can still race around the globe with the best of them. Okay, Fred, let's get down to business. What do you want?"

"I'd like a million dollars, my energetic gasbag."

Ten minutes went by and nothing happened. "What's going on, genie? I said I want a million dollars. Are you hard of hearing or are you welshing on your agreement to give me anything I ask for?"

"I resent the welshing remark, Fred. We genies are scrupulously honest and through the millennia none of us has ever backed down on a promise we've made."

"So what's the deal?"

"You said you'd *like* a million dollars. That's a statement of desire, similar to me wishing to be out of the bottle. You didn't ask me to *get* you a million dollars."

"Very true, my nit-picking pile of vapors. I regret my imprecision. Let me try again. I want you to *get* me a million dollars."

The sky turned dark and the noise was deafening as a hundred million pennies fell to earth around Fred.

"There's your million dollars, master."

Mountains of copper surrounded him. People were running up to these hills of pennies and shoveling handfuls of coins into their pockets and purses. One fellow dialed his wife to come by with a U-Haul truck. Fred's incredulity about the situation quickly turned to anger. "You want to bust my chops. Fine! I'll play word games with you. Listen carefully, my Machiavellian miasma. I want a million dollars deposited to my checking account right now."

Fred barely finished his declaration before he whipped out his cell phone and dialed his bank. After three minutes of being prompted to punch in a pack of numbers, a person popped on the line.

"Can you tell me how much money I have in my checking account?"

"Fourteen dollars and eighty-three cents, sir."

"That's impossible. I should have over a million bucks in the account."

"Let me verify that. Oh, I see what happened. A million-dollar deposit *was* made four minutes ago but it was withdrawn a minute after that. Can I help you with anything else?"

Fred didn't reply. A sick feeling was developing in the pit of his stomach: *Just like a map cannot tell all about the territory, words cannot describe all the things they represent.* He had come across that idea many years ago in a book on general semantics, but he hadn't given the notion much thought. Now the reality of that concept was coming back to haunt him.

Fred gazed up at the genie. "I said I wanted a million dollars in my checking account right now. I guess *right now* meant less than four minutes to you. Am I correct in that assumption?"

"You are, Fred."

The sick feeling in Fred's stomach was getting worse. The genie seemed to know there is always more that one can say about anything; that you can never completely capture a thought or idea through words.

The genie was doing barrel rolls between two fluffy cumulus clouds as Fred began to speak. "Listen up. I have another wish. I want you to put a million dollars into my checking account and let it stay there for a month. Is that clear enough for you?"

"I think it is. But let me paraphrase what you said. You want me to place a million dollars in your checking account and have it remain there for a month."

"You got it, genie."

"No, Fred. You got it."

Fred hit the redial button on his cell phone.

"Customer service, may I help you?"

"I would like to know the current balance in my checking account."

"It is one million fourteen dollars and eighty-three cents, sir."

"Excellent. I am coming down to the bank today to withdraw a portion of that money. Will I have a problem doing this?"

"I'm afraid you will, sir. There's a lien on your account. My records show the million dollars that was deposited contained counterfeit bills. The federal government and our bookkeepers are currently investigating the matter."

Fred threw his phone to the ground and looked up to the firmament.

"I'm stumped, genie. I know that you know what I want, but you keep stopping me from getting things. You're being mean and sadistic. I saved you from a forever bottle cruise. You should be appreciative."

The genie gazed down at Fred and replied, "I was grateful to you for giving me my freedom and wanted very much to repay the favor. But you insisted I grant you multiple wishes even though I told you that doing so would drain genie power to help others in the world. You also acted rudely to me. You said I was an energetic gasbag, you accused me of going back on a promise, and you called me a nit-picking pile of vapors and a Machiavellian miasma. Because I'm not made of solid matter my bones can't be broken, but my feelings can be hurt. You probably assumed they couldn't."

The genie had given him a way out and Fred took it. "You're absolutely right. I thought because your body is ephemeral your emotions would be, too. That was a stupid thing for me to do and I apologize for it. I'm also ashamed of the way I spoke to you. I shouldn't have used such insulting language. Please forgive me."

"I will do that, Fred."

"Thank you, genie. I would very much like to start over. If I speak to you in a respectful manner can I make some more requests?"

"I said I would accede to your wishes and I will not break that promise. But what you are asking of me is immoral. Giving you more wishes stops other people from getting their wishes. Let me make you a counteroffer. I have shown you that no matter how you phrase your requests for things there are ways I can interpret those requests differently from how you meant them because words cannot completely describe everything. As they say in general semantics, there's always an etcetera. Here's what I suggest. Release me from my original promise to give you lots of wishes. Instead, permit me to grant you one thing that you really and truly desire."

Fred reviewed the genie's proposal in his mind but he knew he would agree to the offer. Getting one wish was certainly a lot better than getting none at all.

"Well, genie, there is something that I have always wanted. Ever since I was a child I've had a longing for . . ."

Before he was able to complete his remarks, a strong wind came up and knocked Fred down. As he got up he spied a tornado on the horizon with a large black funnel. It was headed straight for him.

"Oh, my god, I hope I don't get killed out here!" Fred shrieked to no one in particular. "I wish I was safe and sound at home."

Whoosh! Bang! Whoosh!

Fred woke with a startle. He was in his pajamas, lying on his sofa. The television was on. It was after midnight. His cat was meowing for him to come to bed. As Fred rose from the couch to turn off the TV he noticed, through the living room window, what appeared to be a fast-moving cloud in the distance. Although he couldn't be sure, it seemed to be smiling at him and doing loop-de-loops in the moonlit summer sky.

Flo Wright and the Merry Dwarf

F lo Wright was a militant maiden who believed that whatever she wanted she should get. Flo wasn't averse to working hard for what she desired but felt if she put in an effort to make something happen, then it should happen. When things didn't work out the way she wanted them to, Flo flipped out. Her flip-outs raised her blood pressure, brought on migraines, and caused other people to avoid her. They led Flo to lose her job, her boyfriend, and her membership in the Society for World Peace. Even her cat, Fluffy, couldn't take Flo's senseless anger. Fluffy finally ran away when Flo freaked out and burnt the house down because an article she submitted on how to find serenity was rejected by the editors of *Reader's Digest*.

Father Flanagan, the supervisor of the homeless shelter Flo wound up in, tried to help the poor girl control her temper by using a religious angle: "Flo, my dear, anger is one of the seven deadly sins. Try to fight against it."

Alas, try as she might, Flo's attempts to quell the savage beast that raged within her failed. She was expelled from the shelter after she hit a nun with a frying pan for not warning Flo that the soup being served for dinner was very hot. Flo relocated to a six-by-eight-foot plot of grass beside the Brooklyn Bridge.

One morning, from her cardboard box alongside the East River, Flo noticed seven little men bathing in the water. When they finished washing, the munchkins slowly marched past her. She addressed the one who looked the most content.

"I hope you fellows know that the water here is not the cleanest to bathe in."

"We just took a quick dip," the Lilliputian replied. "Thanks for the advice."

"Where are you guys from? You all look vaguely familiar but I can't place the faces."

"Oh, you've probably seen us in the movies or on television. We're the seven dwarfs from the Snow White story."

"What are you guys doing in the Big Apple?" Flo said.

"Disney has released a new DVD of *Snow White*. We're here to promote it," the pint-sized chap responded.

"That's awesome. Which dwarf are you? Doc? Sleepy? Dopey?"

"I'm Grumpy. Pleased to meet you."

"But Grumpy is the angry dwarf. You don't look angry to me."

"I'm not angry," the diminutive fellow retorted, "I'm actually pretty happy. However, I wasn't always happy. For most of my life I was as crabby as the character I play in the movie."

"So what happened? How did you become happy?" Flo asked.

"I've always demanded things go my way but in a talk I attended at the New York Society for General Semantics I learned that *uncertainty* is the norm in life. The speaker specifically spoke about the *General Principle of Uncertainty*."

"What's the General Principle of Uncertainty?"

"The *GPU*, a generalization of the more restricted uncertainty principle of physics, states that because our nervous systems and all events in life are unique, statements describing situations can only be made in terms of probability. For example, 'There's an eighty-five percent likelihood that x will happen,' or 'I am reasonably sure that y will occur.' The fact is, there is very little that is absolutely certain in life. Most things are relative. To stay on an even keel, it's a good idea to learn to live with the 'relatives.'"

"I like that idea," Flo said. "My philosophy has always been that things should happen the way I want them to. I suppose it makes more sense to figure there's only a possibility a thing will occur. Then, if it doesn't happen, you won't get too upset."

"Exactly!" the halfling replied. "I must tell you, probability thinking has helped to make me a cheerful little man."

"You'd never know it from the character you play in *Snow White and the Seven Dwarfs.*"

"Of course you wouldn't know it from that film. My character is supposed to be grumpy so I cheerfully fake that emotion. I'm not stupid. That's Dopey's job."

"I think I'm going to give probability thinking a whirl," Flo said. "I have precious little to lose if it doesn't work and if I can get my anger under control, a whole lot to gain."

"You go, girl," the homunculus responded. "And do me a favor. If you tell people that you've met me, leave out the fact I'm a happy camper. I can't afford to spoil my image. Cartoon characters, unlike human beings, are typecast from the start. The public would never accept a happy Grumpy."

"No problem," the homeless woman answered back. "But I'm definitely going to try to spoil my image. With probability thinking, I intend to be a very happy lady.

A Royal Revelation

King Cruel, a monarch with a moniker that does not suggest mellowness, distrusted his subjects. He thought they were a bunch of boorish malcontents who needed to be constantly whipped into shape. And Cruel took pride in doing the whipping, which took the form of blistering criticisms and withering humiliations. His vitriol and censure produced surly serfs and single-digit popularity ratings.

"The populace does not appreciate me," the king told Seymour, the royal opinion pollster. "I know I often act harshly toward the underlings, but it is for their own good and that of the realm. They are a lazy, mindless group of clods and nothing would ever get done around the empire if it wasn't for my continuous goading."

"Your Highness," Seymour replied, "are you familiar with the notion of *logical fate?*"

The king was not conversant with that concept and asked Seymour to clue him in on it.

"Logical fate, an idea popularized by Alfred Korzybski, the founder of general semantics, involves the idea that consequences follow assumptions. Since you assume that you are the leader of a pack of indolent, good-for-nothing vassals who have to be prodded and chastised at every opportunity, you treat them disdainfully. But your assumptions may be wrong. Have you ever considered that?"

"No, I haven't, Sy. My dad imbued me with the thought that

human beings don't want to work and to get them to do anything you have to bust their chops. I have diligently followed that philosophy."

"Well, Sire, maybe it's time you checked things out for yourself. Are you up for a little experiment?"

The king liked experiments. One of his favorite ways to relax was to mix chemicals in the royal laboratory.

"Sure. What do you have in mind?"

"To get a better handle on what makes the people tick, I suggest you shed the royal robes, don some street gear, and mix in with the masses for a couple of months."

"That's a great idea, Sy. Undercover work has always intrigued me. I'll begin today." The king thereupon went off to lunch, shed his royal robes for jeans and a t-shirt, and left the palace for a royal adventure.

As he roamed the realm, Cruel observed many of the chattel were cheating on their taxes and not putting in a full day's work for a full day's pay. When he asked the drudges why they were acting this way he was told it was because of the king's meanness and lack of sensitivity when he spoke to them. "We wouldn't mind working hard and paying what the state demands in taxes," a number of the grubs told him, "but the king gets off on dissing us, so we dis him right back."

When his investigation was finished Cruel returned to the palace. He felt confused and sad: *I need a more effective plan for ruling the rabble. I think I'll send for Seymour.*

When Seymour arrived at the royal chambers the king said, "Sy, I have come to realize that my assumptions concerning human relations have not been good ones. They have cost the royal coffers much revenue and have contributed to the kingdom's lousy GNP. I need to alter my assumptions and ways to communicate with the denizens of my dominion."

Seymour replied, "Some of the best hypotheses on how to improve human relations have been offered by Dale Carnegie, the author of *How to Win Friends and Influence People*. Millions of individuals have used his suggestions on how to get along well with others to positive effect. Here are a few of his recommendations: If you like something that someone does, tell them about it. To motivate individuals to work with you, take a genuine interest in their desires. If you are right and the other person is wrong, do not publicly humiliate them for the error, let the other person save face."

The king thanked Seymour for his advice and he replaced his old ideas about how to deal with people with those of Dale Carnegie. As a result he got along much better with the commoners. They worked harder and paid their fair share of taxes. The king's popularity soared. A petition went around requesting that the king change his name from King Cruel to King Kind. Because the alliteration was the same, and because kings get what kings want, the Royal Department of Name Changes approved the new handle.

King Kind went on to become one of the most cared for and respected rulers in the history of the monarchy. It was not uncommon for his subjects to wait on line in front of the palace for hours just to receive a royal handshake or a royal pat on the head for doing good work. When King Kind died, statues with his likeness were erected throughout the kingdom and a national holiday was proclaimed in his honor. All this because the man was wise enough to consider the notion of logical fate and ditch poor conjectures for better ones.

Don't Worry, Be Happy

In a land where five percent of the world's population consumes a quarter of the world's oil, there lived a business executive named Bob who had no patience for things that couldn't be done quickly and easily. And he wasn't the only American who felt this way. Many social scientists say that the increased watching of television, with its fast-changing images and sounds, and the proliferation of modern timesaving devices that make tasks easier to complete, has led to an expansion of low frustration tolerance in the United States.

One morning, when Bob was home eating a breakfast of instant oatmeal, instant coffee, and an instant breakfast bar, he received an instant message from his boss, Mel Moneygrubber. "An urgent matter has come up. I need to see you right away." Bob jumped into his two-gallon-to-the-mile SUV and headed for work.

Moneygrubber was pacing nervously when Bob entered his office. "Bob, the latest quarterly report shows our company didn't make the profits that I promised our shareholders. What's going on?"

Bob, who was the comptroller for the Moneygrubber Oil Corporation, replied, "A substantial sum of money was diverted to research and development last quarter. That's why profits are lower, sir."

"I don't give a hoot about research and development," Moneygrubber said. "I want profits now. Who authorized putting money into R&D?"

"I don't know, boss, but I'll look into it *tout suite*."

"You had better. Let me know when you find out something. And stop using French expressions. I can barely understand you when you speak to me in English."

Bob went back to his office. "Ms. Robins," Bob said to his secretary, "call R&D and tell them that I want to see Mr. Jenkins immediately."

Jenkins, the head of the company's R&D department, came at once. "What can I do for you, Bob?"

"Mr. Moneygrubber is up in arms about not reaching last quarter's profit goals. Did you ask the finance department to transfer money from the company's interest-bearing slush fund account to your department?"

"I did indeed, Bob. And they approved it."

"Are you nuts? You know the philosophy here—profits today, tomorrow will take care of itself. We don't waste extra bucks on research and development."

"I'm a team player, Bob, and though I believe our company's policy to not invest heavily in R&D is penny wise and pound foolish I've always gone along with it. But I've been thinking that oil is a finite resource that will eventually run out, so it makes sense to do research and development now to come up with alternative energy sources before that happens."

"Jenkins, the public doesn't care about oil running out. If they did, people would be using public transportation more, turning air-conditioners off when leaving the room, and drinking water from paper cups instead of plastic bottles. Our shareholders want to make money chop-chop; they're happy to let their kids and grandkids worry about alternative fuels."

"Why should future generations be saddled with that problem, Bob? We should be searching for alternative energy sources today, while we have a bit of an energy cushion. And, there's another thing to consider. The quicker we find a substitute for oil, the quicker we can pull out of areas of the world that are rife with terrorism."

"Terrorism doesn't bother people as much as not having things when they want them, Jenkins. We live in an age of immediate gratification. Folks want to feel good in the moment. That's why people watch television, eat at McDonald's, and pay others to wait on line for them at Disney World. Americans want happiness without delay, ASAP, pronto."

"Well, Alfred Korzybski, the founder of general semantics, had a different formula for happiness. He said the best way to reach that condition was through realistic goal-setting and hard work. That's how people have made progress through the ages. Setting credible goals and working hard to achieve them leads folks to live more satisfying lives and to be better off in the long run."

"When it comes to the long run, Jenkins, I subscribe to the philosophy of John Maynard Keynes who said, 'in the long run we are all dead.' I sure hope this guy Korzybski can figure a way for you and your family to survive on unemployment insurance because if you keep hunting for alternative fuels you are going to be out of a job."

"Don't worry about me, Bob. I'll be all right. If Moneygrubber fires me I'm going to join some professors I know at the university and work with them on developing new energy sources. Even if I'm kept on I intend to grind away at such ventures in my spare time, because that will make me happy and it may have good results for humanity. By the way, there's a ton of dough to be made in developing alternative fuels."

"You're an idealist, Jenkins, but it seems to me that there's some sense in what you've been saying. So, for the sake of moving this story in the direction the author would like it to go, and because I like making money, I am going to hedge my bets and give you some moolah for your alternative energy research projects. How does ten thousand dollars sound?"

"Sounds good to me, Bob. That investment is going to pay you and your progeny big dividends. If it turns out oil is contributing to global warming, you may even be helping to save the planet. How about we go to lunch downtown and celebrate your wise decision to invest in the future. I'll drive."

"Thanks for the offer, Jenkins, but I'd rather eat at the diner across the street. The food is pretty good there but more importantly, why waste money on burning gas. Besides, until you or somebody else comes up with a practical alternative to oil, conserving a non-renewable source of energy may not be a bad thing to do. And I could use the exercise. How about when we finish lunch we walk around the block a few times."

"I'm walking with you already, Bob, down the general semantics path of hard work and perseverance to create a better world for people who are alive today and for generations yet to come."

Charlie and the Reality Fairy

C harlie Chinwagger, like so many others who inhabit the third rock from the sun, was, in general semantics parlance, an *intensionally orientated* individual. Such a person tends to rely on abstract verbal definitions about what is going on in the world. He believed in meaningless mumbo jumbo: "Try Britesmile toothpaste. New! With dynachlorosyl." He used gobbledygook at work: "Pupil placement and articulation procedures should amalgamate and aggregate a diverse and assorted amount of data and dada to produce relevant information." And he practiced verbal magic: "If I think a movie is great, it is great." Charlie's over-reliance on words to derive meaning made him oblivious to reality.

Then reality bit him. To be more precise, his neighbor's dog, Friendly, whom Charlie had always believed to be a kind canine because of his name, took a chunk out of Chuck's leg. When Charlie complained to Friendly's owner about the incident the fellow replied, "Why did you try to pet Friendly when he was running around my yard? Didn't the fact that I put a muzzle on him when we go out for walks mean anything to you? And you've seen the mailman unholster his dog repellent when he delivers mail to my house."

When Charlie went to the office the next morning, reality once more reared its ugly head. His boss, Ken Candid, told him that Sal Suckupski was being appointed head of the department of educational evaluation. Charlie had thought that post was going to be his.

"Ken, I was taught that those who work hard and play by the rules advance in their careers. I did those things, yet Suckupski, who didn't, is being promoted. There's something wrong with that."

"Charlie, I am going to be candid with you," Candid countered. "The road to advancement around here is through office politics. Suckupski is a master in that area. If you want to get ahead in this organization you better revise your theoretical notions about how one moves up the ladder in bureaucracies and take into account what is happening in the place where you are actually working."

When Charlie came home that night he told his wife about his not being promoted, and reality bit him once again.

"Charlie, I'm having an affair with Tom, the guy who lives in the apartment across the hall. I'm leaving you."

Charlie was taken aback by his wife's declaration. Then, after shattering all the dishes in the kitchen, overturning a La-Z-Boy recliner and an oversized couch in the living room, and screaming so loudly that the police were called to come to his house, he composed himself and said, "Chastity, I don't believe this is happening. How long have you been having this affair?"

"For a little over a year," his wife replied. "I thought you knew about it. I figured you put two and two together when you discovered Tom's underwear under our bed. In fact, I thought you knew about our trysts even earlier than that. For example, when you came across Tom and me having drinks at the Cuckold Lounge three months ago or when you found Tom's love letter to me on our kitchen table right after that."

Charlie silently counted to a hundred before responding. Then he said, "Tom's letter led me to believe Tom liked you, but I didn't think you were having an affair. And I thought you were having drinks with Tom to bolster his confidence in talking to women. You told me he's shy and has trouble getting dates. As for Tom's underwear, I assumed he had left his briefs in a dryer in the laundry room and when you were doing our laundry it simply got mixed in."

"Charlie, do you know what the word 'clueless' means?"

"Yes, I do, and I think that's what I am."

When he got up the next morning and went into the bathroom to shave, Charlie was surprised to find a small imaginary being with magical powers and a human form sitting opposite him atop the medicine cabinet.

"Who are you?" Charlie asked.

"My name is Clinker Bell. I am a reality fairy. You can call me Clink."

"What is a reality fairy?"

"A reality fairy tries to help humans who are out of it, get back into it. To be more precise, a reality fairy provides people with useful tips and ideas on how to solve everyday problems."

"Wow!" Charlie exclaimed, "I can't believe I'm talking to a fairy. This whole situation seems unreal."

"It would be if this were an academic treatise or a nonfiction work of literature," the sprite responded, "but as this is a fairy tale, the situation you find yourself in is perfectly plausible."

"So, Clink, how did you know I needed help?"

"Fairyland Central monitors human behavior and cognition. When an individual reaches a dangerous level of unreality, a call goes out to a reality fairy to provide aid to that person. You hit your level when you were denied that promotion at work."

"Geez, I've never heard of reality fairies but then I never knew that Disney World is actually larger than seventeen different countries. Okay, Clink, in what way can you assist me?"

"I can supply you with guidelines for what is known in general semantics as *extensional thinking*," the pixie replied.

"What's extensional thinking?"

"It's an attitude toward living that involves orienting oneself primarily to the facts."

"I would like to orient myself that way," Charlie said. "Go ahead, hit me with your best stuff."

"I'll be glad to. Rule number one: Check the map—your experiences, images, and words, against the territory—the experiences, images, and words it represents. For example, a dog named Friendly is not necessarily a friendly dog."

"That's true," Charlie replied. "And a wife named Chastity is not necessarily a virtuous woman."

"Rule number two: Use the scientific method (observe, test, evaluate) to solve everyday problems. Had you done that with respect to your efforts at career advancement you wouldn't have been sandbagged by Suckupski."

"True again," Charlie said. "I would have noticed what was going on in the office and used different strategies to get ahead there."

"Rule number three: To make accurate assessments of situations, and to avoid jumping to wrong conclusions about them, learn how to distinguish facts from inferences. Factual statements are made *after* observation or experience, are confined to what one observes or experiences, and represent a high degree of probability. If you had focused on the facts vis-à-vis your wife's behavior with Tom, you might have figured out what they were up to."

"I bet I would have," Charlie said. "These rules are great. I can't wait to put them into practice. Do you have any other guidelines for me?"

"I do, but unfortunately I can't stay here any longer. I just received an urgent text message to go to Washington, DC. Fairyland Central has determined that the president and Congress are so out of touch with reality that the republic is in danger. If you want more information on extensional thinking I suggest you contact the Institute of General Semantics."

"How do I do that?"

"Google the Institute on your computer. So long, Charlie. I wish you the best and, as they used to tell us back in training, 'Keep it real!'"

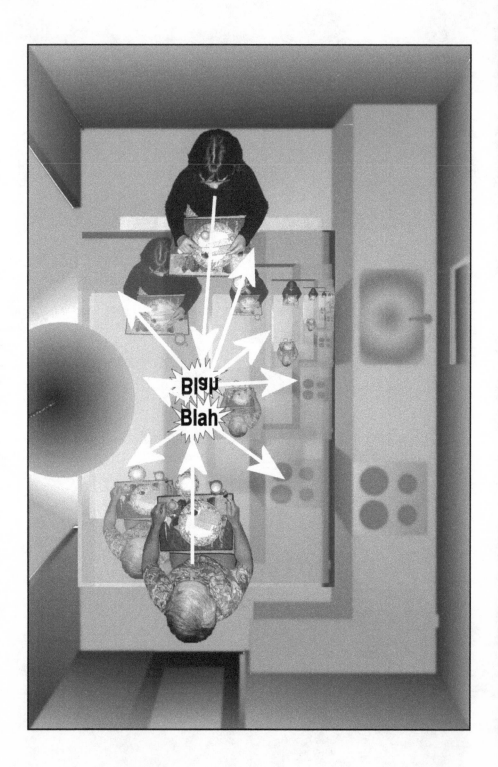

Professor Postman Brings
Home the Bacon

In a lovely little village where the flowers bloom, birdies chirp, and butterflies flutter by fragrant fields of forsythias and forget-me-nots, there lived a young couple by the name of Jen and Jerry. The two "J"s, like lots of other people in the contiguous forty-eight states and Alaska and Hawaii, existed in a state of language unawareness. A crucial characteristic of people with this condition is a propensity to employ what NYU professor and general semantics expert Neil Postman labels "stupid talk." Such talk is typified by a confused direction, an inappropriate tone, or words not well suited to their context. Stupid talk does not or cannot achieve its aims.[1]

Let's look in at Jen and Jerry at the start of a typical day.

It is seven in the morning. Jen enters the kitchen. She sits down and says, "Good morning." Her husband says the same. Then he places some bacon and eggs before her. She starts to eat.

Jen: The bacon is a little crisp this morning.

Jerry: What?

Jen: The bacon—it's way too crisp.

---

[1] This fairy tale and some of the dialogue in it was inspired by Neil Postman's brilliant book *Crazy Talk, Stupid Talk* (New York: Delacorte, 1976).

Jerry: I always make it that way.

Jen: Not this way. It's too crisp. Almost burnt.

Jerry: Really? Why don't you make it yourself! Then, you can have the bacon just the way *you want*.

Jen: Why don't you get a job in an office somewhere! Then you can earn a salary and have the money *you want*.

Jerry: You don't call what I do a job? Writing novels is hard work. As a matter of fact, it's damn hard work. I face blank pages every day and have to fill them with original thoughts.

Jen: How about this for an original thought: go to cooking school and learn how to make bacon that's fit for human beings to eat.

Jerry: How about you go to a school that teaches people to be grateful for those who make meals for them and clean around the house.

Jen: I don't have time to go a school like that because I have to travel into town to work every day. Someone in this family has got to make dough to pay the bills around here.

Jerry: We made a deal when we got married that I would do the housework and write at home and you would practice law in the city. I'm keeping up on my end of the bargain but if you want to renegotiate our agreement that's fine with me. In the meantime, I hope you choke on your bacon.

Perhaps we should leave the kitchen now, before the pots and pans get thrown about the room.

Jen and Jerry had been having arguments like the one just described for several years and they did not make for conjugal bliss. One night, after a particularly truculent blow-up, Jen decided she would take action against the stupid talk marring the happy relationship she wished to have with her spouse. The next day she telephoned Neil Postman, whom she had met when Postman gave a talk at a local library about ways to communicate more effectively.

After explaining the bacon brouhaha to Postman, Jen said, "I want to stop having fights with my husband that spin out of control. Can you give me some advice on how to do that?"

"Sure," Postman replied. "Communication is tricky. We may

think we are talking about something simple, like bacon being too crisp, but 'too crisp' is a matter of interpretation. Every nervous system is unique and will experience 'crispness' in its own way. Furthermore, as general semanticists are fond of pointing out, people will often respond not only to the subject matter of our remarks, but to our *remarks*, as well.[1] They may not like, for example, our point of view or form of address. And so, they say something that refers in part to the gist of our remarks—like, in the example you gave me, to the condition of the bacon—and in part to how they interpreted our message.

"When it is our turn to speak, instead of focusing on the condition of the bacon, we respond to the attacks on us. Before long, the particulars concerning two slices of perhaps overcooked bacon, have been relegated to the waste heap, and our comments are solely driven by comments that are far from the topic that we were originally discussing."

"I completely get what you're saying," Jen said. "I bugged out when Jerry told me he always makes bacon the same way and said stupid stuff about wanting him to get a conventional job, which I know he would hate. That was clearly a mistake."

"It most assuredly was, Jen. The situation was doing all the talking here, and to the extent that you and Jerry could not fend off what was happening or redirect it, you were both engaging in stupid talk, which you both were almost certain to regret at a later date. It is nearly always a problem when a semantic process has gotten going and you do not know how it started, and, most especially, how to stop it."

"That makes total sense to me, Professor Postman. You're the *man*! And I intend to be the *wo*man by applying what you've said to keep me from engaging in stupid talk with my husband."

The snippet of dialogue that follows, which occurred a few days later, is evidence that Jen is being successful in her goal.

Jen: I find the bacon a little crisp this morning.

Jerry: What?

Jen: The bacon seems a bit crisp.

---

[1] The idea that there can be words about words about words, etc. is labeled *self-reflexiveness* in general semantics parlance.

Jerry: I always make it that way.

Jen: Gee, I must be getting old or something. I never noticed. Do you think it might be possible for you to make me another couple of slices a little less crisp?

Jerry: I think I could do that.

The Meaning of Words

In a land beautiful for spacious skies and amber waves of grain, for purple mountains' majesty above the fruited plains, there lived a hard-working, god-fearing woman named Ava. This archetypal American went to work, paid her taxes, and listened to political discussions on talk radio, where she heard comments like: "Liberals are not patriotic!" "Conservatives are mean!" "All politicians are crooks!" Ava, and millions of her fellow citizens, believed labeling individuals in such ways fosters political discourse.

One day, Ava attended a rally where she heard speeches from people with different political backgrounds. The "liberal" speaker was a fellow who had served in the military with great distinction and he spoke lovingly about the country. The "conservative" speaker headed a large charity and spent her weekends, as a volunteer, building houses for the poor. Both speakers were incumbent officeholders who had been praised in numerous editorials and news stories for their conscientiousness and dedication in serving the needs of their constituents.

When she went home that evening, Ava thought about what she had heard at the political rally. The liberal speaker seemed quite patriotic and the conservative speaker very altruistic. Ava concluded that labels can be at odds with reality. She also concluded that she would stop listening to political talk-radio shows.

At 9 p.m. the phone rang. It was Ava's boyfriend Avi. He was calling to say that he was ending his five-year relationship with her because he was in love with someone else. Ava was dumbfounded at hearing this because Avi had repeatedly told Ava he was in love with her.

When Ava got off the phone she took Avi's picture from her wallet and tore it to shreds. Then she called Avi's boss, Andy, and left a message saying Avi had told Ava that he was embezzling funds from the company. Then she made herself a cup of tea and reflected on Avi's duplicity and his use of the word "love." *It seems that different people can define the same word differently. It also seems that Avi is a two-timing, good-for-nothing, double-talking rat.*

Ava found it difficult to get to sleep that night. A jigger of scotch, three Valiums, two Seconals, and a cup of warm milk did not help her to find peaceful repose. They took her to a different place.

"Where am I?" Ava asked the specter who appeared before her.

"You're in Wonderland," the apparition replied.

"You mean the Wonderland from the Alice story?"

"No, not that Wonderland. You're in a cerebral realm that lies somewhere between Consciousness and Blottoville."

"How did I get here?"

"Drugs and alcohol were the vehicle, your imagination was the driver."

"What goes on in Wonderland?"

"All sorts of things, and a lot of them depend on you. For example, what's on your mind right now?"

"Well, my belief in language has been severely shaken. I always thought words had meaning. But I've discovered in politics and romance that's not necessarily true. It makes me think words really don't have meaning."

The phantom roared with laughter, then he composed himself and began to speak. "Strictly speaking, *words* don't mean, *people* mean. Don't ask, 'What does word X mean?' Ask instead, 'What do I mean when I say word X?' or 'What do you mean when you say word X?' The fact is, words do not have one true meaning. The three-letter-word *run*, just for the verb-form alone, has no fewer than 645 meanings listed in *The Oxford English Dictionary*. Words mean different things to different people. Words mean different things at different times. Words mean different things in different contexts."

Ava was deeply discomfited by the phantasm's remarks. She had always thought objective meaning could be found in words. But this ghoul was demolishing that proposition. She wondered what else this language maven would say. She didn't have to wait long to find out.

"What's the difference between a 'freedom fighter' and a 'terrorist?' When prison guards beat prisoners and pour cold water on them are the detainees being subject to 'abuse' or 'torture?' Are organizations that comment on news reporting 'media watchdog groups' or are they 'pressure groups?' Don't look to the dictionary for the answers to these questions. Their answers depend on how individuals interpret people and situations."

"You know so much about language," Ava said to the spook. "Are you an English professor?"

"No," the wraith replied. "I am a student of general semantics, a discipline that helps me to think about language in important and practical ways. For example, I used to imagine that labeling people was a smart way to think about politics. But I learned through general semantics that doing this does not provide wisdom on political matters. It leads instead to *hardening of the categories*, an illness that is rampant today in America."

"Can that condition be cured?" Ava asked the ghost.

"It can be beaten through a rational analysis of the issues and carefully scrutinizing the words we use to classify and identify people and events. The categories we devise are not 'out there,' in the 'real world.' They are created in our heads and expressed in language. How we label or categorize a person depends upon our purposes, our projections, and our evaluations."

"That's a very sensible view," Ava said to her illusionary acquaintance. "I hope I'll have a memory of it when I leave Wonderland."

"I'm sure you will," the revenant replied. "You heard the information contained in my linguistic philosophy two weeks ago, the night Avi took you to a talk on the meaning of meaning that was sponsored by the New York Society for General Semantics. You weren't paying much attention to the speaker that evening, but a lot of what he was saying made its way to your subconscious mind. It's actually his words that have been coming out of my mouth."

Ava rolled over in her bed, started to mumble, and began to flail around. This was behavior she typically displayed when she was about to wake up from a dream.

"Uh oh, it looks like you're gaining consciousness so I better go. But before I leave I want to say that I've really enjoyed chatting with you. And for what it's worth, I'm glad you're rid of Avi. I always thought he was an impostor and a no-good skunk."

All That Jazz

Megan Miller was raised in a high-energy nuclear family. Sadly, much of that energy was focused on finding fault with her. Megan was constantly told she wasn't very smart, she wasn't very pretty, she lacked personality, and she would never amount to much.

After dropping out of high school, Megan took a job as a dog walker. The money she made from that vocation went to buying drugs for herself and Hulk Harmon, her verbally and physically abusive boyfriend. She ignored her appearance, ate too much, and felt as lousy as she looked.

Megan tried to find solace by confiding in her friends. That didn't work out too well. When Megan told her best friend, Penny, that she was feeling miserable and depressed because her parents kept telling her that she was stupid, lazy, and rotten, Penny replied, "Don't be sad. You may be stupid and lazy but I don't think you're rotten. Have a drink. It will cheer you up."

Megan liked to drink, but the booze provided only short-term pain relief and it was interfering with her work and social life. Some of Megan's customers had terminated their contracts with her because she sometimes showed up drunk to walk their dogs. And Hulk, who was a teetotaler, was demanding Megan refrain from alcohol and stick to drugs. Her life was a mess.

Megan was about to order her fifth gin and tonic from Brad the bartender in the Gallows' End Tavern when a short fellow with horn-rimmed glasses and a pencil-thin mustache sitting next to her began to speak.

"I'm in town for a few days and I want to catch some good music. Do you know if there are any decent jazz clubs in this city?"

"I know some excellent jazz clubs," Megan replied. "Actually, I'm a big jazz fan. When I'm not drinking or taking drugs I love to listen to jazz. Why don't I accompany you to a jazz club tonight."

"That would be great," the man responded. "I'd be happy to pick you up in my car. What time shall we meet?"

"You can stop by my apartment at 8 p.m."

"I'll be there. Until then, I suggest you confine your drinking to Shirley Temples. If you wish, I'll buy you stronger stuff at the club tonight."

"Okay. By the way, mister, what's your name?"

"S.I. Hayakawa."

When Megan and Hayakawa arrived at *The Jazz House* Megan went to the bar and ordered a gin and tonic.

"Why do you drink so much, Megan?"

"I'm a poorly educated, part-time dog walker with a drugged-out boyfriend and no future. My parents said I would never amount to anything and they were right. I see no reason to stay sober."

"That seems like a lot of jazz to me," Hayakawa said, "and I don't mean the kind we're listening to now."

"You can't argue with the truth. I'm a failure and I'll always be a failure."

"Megan, thinking oneself a 'failure' is an inference that can negatively impact one's ability to learn and perform well. If you believe you are a failure you will begin to act that way and so create a condition known as a 'self-fulfilling prophecy.' If you strongly believe the labels you give yourself, you may also behave in ways that will create 'other-fulfilling prophecies' and have people act towards you as if the labels you have given yourself are true."

"Wow, that's intense," Megan said. "Are you a psychologist?"

"No. I'm a student of general semantics, a discipline that is concerned with how people use words, and how words use people. I can tell you as a practitioner of general semantics that little good can come from categorizing oneself a 'failure' or using other sorts of pejorative labeling."

"Judging from my case, I'd have to agree with you. Thinking myself a failure hasn't helped me to move ahead in life but it's become a habit. Do you have any suggestions on how I can rectify that situation?"

"I think you should concentrate your thoughts and energy on particular areas in your life that are giving you trouble. I'm a college professor and when students tell me what big failures they are, I tell them to zero in on particulars such as 'How can I improve my grades?' or 'What can I do to have friends?' When they whine over the 'fact' that they are 'naturally' lazy, I tell my students to set their alarm clocks and schedule their days."

"Have your students been helped by those ideas?"

"Many have. Taking action on problems often leads people to make inroads into solving them and it can help increase awareness that words like 'failure,' 'stupid,' and 'lazy' are not objective categories that exist in the world. Rather, they are subjective human evaluations and, as such, need to be rigorously examined before being accepted as true."

"That's an interesting thought, Professor Hayakawa. For as long as I can remember, I've considered myself a failure. I figured I was being objective in that conclusion, but I guess I was just making a destructive self-inference. What I should have done was focus on how to improve my life in specific ways."

"It's never too late to begin doing that, Megan. You can start to work on making improvements to your life right now."

"Can you recommend any books to assist me with that?"

"Take a look at the latest edition of *Language in Thought and Action*.[1] I wrote that book to help people overcome problems through the use of general semantics, a science-based "self-help" system designed

---

[1] S.I. Hayakawa, *Language in Thought in Action: Fifth Edition*. (New York: Harvest, 1991). Originally published in 1941 as *Language in Action*.

to help individuals gain a more accurate picture of themselves and the world in which they live."

"Thanks, professor. I'll get your book. By the way, what do you think of the music here?"

"I'm enjoying it tremendously. It's like you: mellow but with an edge."

The following day Megan went to the public library and asked the librarian if Hayakawa's book was available for loan.

"It is," the librarian replied, "and I think you'll enjoy it. I read *Language in Thought and Action* when I was in college during the nineteen-eighties."

"That's odd," Megan said. "I was with the author last night and he seemed to be a fairly young guy."

"You must be joking. S.I. Hayakawa died over twenty-five years ago. There is no way you could have been with him last night."

Megan was astounded by the librarian's words. Who was the fellow she had gone out with? Was it Hayakawa's ghost? Was her escort a mental patient? Could he have been a practical joker who knew something about general semantics? Whoever the guy was, he had saved her life and given her hope. He had made her see the important role that language plays in shaping one's attitudes and decisions. With this knowledge she could overcome her parents' harmful conditioning. She could work on getting a GED and then a college degree. Megan was jazzed. By golly, she was going to stop drinking and amount to something.

Alfred's Reality Map

In a city so nice they named it twice, there lived a gallant young fellow named Tony Nobaloney who was always looking for new and better ways to think about things.

On a warm summer afternoon, as Tony was walking through Times Square to buy tickets to a Broadway show, he saw a young woman chasing a sheet of pink paper being blown by the wind. The woman was shouting, "Help, help, I need that paper. It's very important. If I don't bring it to my boss he'll fire me." Tony yelled back to her "Don't worry, I'll get it." He then ran after the paper and grabbed it by an open manhole, which he unfortunately fell into.

When Tony regained consciousness, he found himself in a beautiful meadow that had in it wildflowers, bees, and a bunch of motionless cows. When he tried to touch one of the animals his hand went right through it, as if it wasn't there. "How can that be?" he muttered. "Cows are solid objects. A hand just can't pass through them."

A voice responded, "That's what all the people say."

"Who are you?" Tony asked a short, stocky fellow who surfaced beside him.

"I'm the groundskeeper here. My name is Alfred. What's your name?"

"My name is Tony. Where am I?"

"You're in the land of Reality. If you want a map of the territory

it'll cost you five bucks. The money is used to provide for the cows."
Tony forked over a fiver and in return received a hand-drawn sketch
that had on it a U-shaped line connected to a circle followed by a
vertical row of three squares and the word ETCETERA.

Alfred's Reality Map

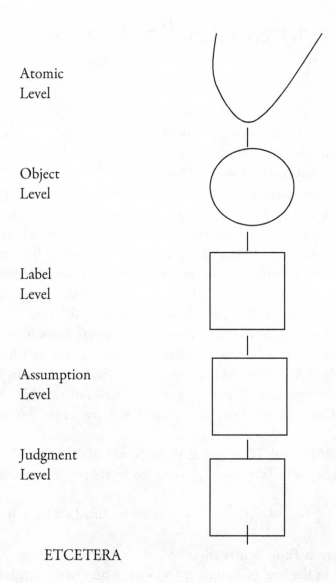

Atomic
Level

Object
Level

Label
Level

Assumption
Level

Judgment
Level

ETCETERA

"This is the strangest map I've ever seen, Alfred. I don't understand it."

"This map is a guide to understanding the world. Let me start with the parabola, the U-shaped figure at the top of the map.

"The parabola represents the *atomic level*. That's a level concerned with atoms and subatomic particles that can't be seen with the naked eye. People think they are looking at solid, fixed objects but that's not accurate. Consider a cow. A cow, like everything else in the world, is composed of atoms whizzing all around. We may call it a cow, a noun, but what is really happening is 'cowing,' a verb that indicates all the atoms and particles of the cow are continually in motion."

Tony found Alfred's account of the atomic level *udderly* fascinating and he thought it had been framed quite *cow*herently. "So, Alfred, I suppose you could call a cup *cupping*, a can *canning*, a table *tabling*, and, if I may use a witticism, a kid could be called *kidding*."

"You got it, Tony, but I've heard that joke before."

"From who?"

"From other people who have come here."

"So other people have been here besides me?"

"Oh, yes. Other people have fallen into Reality. Let's move down to the *object* level, a level where things can be seen. On this level, people can look at a cow, a goat, a sheep, a bowl of chicken soup, an Alfred Hitchcock movie, a portrait of Whistler's mother or indeed anything in the world but because everyone's nervous system is different they will focus on different features. For example, in the case of a cow, one person may notice that the cow has no tail and the other that the cow has tiny brown markings by their ear. The fact is, no two people will see an object in the exact same way and our senses are not sensitive enough to take in everything about an object."

"Given that last point, Alfred, I think it is reasona*bull* to conclude that what goes on at the object level is not all that objective."

"That's *cow*rect, Tony. On to the *label level*! Let's put a nametag on our hypothetical cow and call her 'Chloe' and let's label her a brown, sixteen-hundred-pound heifer that likes to push her way to the front of the queue at feeding time and *bulldoze* fences till they give way.

Please note the name is not the object, it merely stands for the object, and when we label something, whether it's 'brown,' 'sixteen hundred pounds,' 'a heifer,' or 'pushy' we are leaving out many of the other characteristics that make up the object."

Tony slapped at a fly buzzing around his head and thought *if I had to give this creature a label I would call it a "damn pest."*

"Shall we proceed to the *assumption level*, Tony?"

"Certainly. Lead on Macduff."

"My name is Alfred not Macduff."

"It seems you're stuck on the label level but I will accept your correction. Lead on, Alfred."

"At the *assumption level* we can make conjectures about cows based on what we have read about or seen. For example, many people assume that cows have four stomachs because they read it somewhere. The fact is cows have one stomach with four chambers. And many folks assume that it is the red color of the cape that causes bulls to charge. In actuality, bovines are red-green colorblind. It is the motion of the cape that angers bulls and leads them to charge not the color. The point of these examples is that statements made on the assumption level—because they are based on conjectures rather than 'objective' facts—need to be carefully checked out and verified before being accepted as true."

Tony thought the notion of verifying and checking out assumptions was a good idea and that is why he said to Alfred, "When I first saw the cows down here I assumed they were real. But they must be hologram cows since you can put your hands through them. Am I right about that?"

"You are, Tony. I use these holographic cows as teaching devices. They cost me almost nothing to maintain and I like the way they look. Their only downsides are they don't produce milk and if I tried to cook hamburgers with them I'd basically be eating the bun."

"That's very *bunny*, Alfred, but I want to know about the next level so *cud* we please *moove* on."

"No problem. At the *judgment level* we are becoming more general in our remarks. For example, we may say, 'cows are sweet animals' or 'cows are lazy animals' or 'cows are cute.' Such remarks are based on our experience, knowledge, and feelings about cows and these statements may or may not have validity for any particular cow."

Tony mused that if cows ran the world, human beings would be the ones being judged and categorized and he wondered what sorts of arbitrary comments the cows would make about them—maybe an overweight female cow would be called "a human" and if a cow overreacted to a situation one might say "don't have a human." It was an intriguing idea but before he could give the matter more thought Alfred began to speak about the ETCETERA at the bottom of the map.

"The ETCETERA is meant to suggest that there are additional levels to follow, to wit, we can keep making ever more general and wide-ranging statements about cows. We can refer to cows as *farm assets*, or just *assets*, or even *wealth*. With these descriptions we are getting farther away from knowing specific information about Chloe, the cow that we en*cow*ntered on the label level."

Tony thought labeling Chloe a *farm asset* or an *asset* or a form of *wealth* changed her from an animal he could envision into a highly abstract generalization. It was his experience that people often mistook such generalizations for actual things and he told that to Alfred who replied, "People do it all the time. For example, people talk about *nations* as if they were real things but there is no objective test to tell if some entity is a 'nation,' no universal agreement on how to define a 'nation.' Other notions that are vaguer than they appear include *the id, ego, and superego*; *the mind*, and *intelligence*."

The fly that had been flitting around Tony's head made another foray and Tony swiped at it and missed. Frustrated, he thought *how can these tiny insects with their infinitesimally small brains outwit people so easily? It's too bad the flies in Reality aren't hologram figures like the cows.*

Alfred saw that Tony was distracted and asked him if everything was okay.

"I'm fine. I was just thinking that your map seems to be describing how people process information in the world where I come from."

"It does, my friend. I lived in that world for the first half of the twentieth century and at that time drew a different and somewhat more comprehensive map about how people process information. I called that map the *Structural Differential*[1] and used it to discuss general semantics, a system I developed to help individuals better understand themselves and their surroundings. Since I've left the land of the living and materialized as a fairy-tale character, I spend my days instructing those who fall down the manhole about how to make sense of the world."

"I'd love to find out more about the Structural Differential. Do you have any suggestions on how I can do that?"

"I noticed on a pink-colored flier that I found next to you when you were unconscious that the New York Society for General Semantics is sponsoring a lecture tonight on that very topic at the main branch of the New York Public Library. You might be interested to know that on the back of the flier there were penciled-in stock market quotations with words that said, "Buy these stocks now, they're about to hit the roof.""

"Do you have that flier, Alfred?"

"Yes, would you like it?"

"I sure would. I think it's going to make a woman I met right before I came down here very happy. Her boss really wanted to see that flier, probably because of the stock tips."

"Is that woman going to attend the general semantics lecture tonight?"

"I don't think so but I would like to go to that talk. I never thought about the physical world and language in the way you've mapped it out. I find your ideas on the subject really interesting. I just need to figure out how to get back to my old life to tell people about those ideas."

"That shouldn't be a problem. Try clicking your heels, or making a wish, or calling an Uber to pick you up. If none of those things work, I am sure the author of this story will devise a way to get you out of here. However, I must go now or I'll be late for dinner, but I can tell you

---

[1] See https://en.wikipedia.org/wiki/Structural_differential

this: I may not be the world's greatest expert on gastronomy but I do know something about reality, and it's the only place to get a decent meal."

Nathan's Nebulous Questions

Nathan and Norman were identical twins who were so much
alike people couldn't tell them apart. That is, until they
began to speak.

Nathan constantly asked questions that couldn't be answered—
for example, "Why was I born?" "Will I be a success?" "Can I truly be
happy?" His parents, teachers, and friends tried to answer his questions
but since there was no way of ascertaining any particular response as
valid, their replies always fell short in Nathan's mind.

Norman didn't ask nebulous questions. Rather than asking why
he was born, Norman asked, "What biological processes caused my
birth?" Instead of speculating on whether or not he would be
successful, Norman concentrated on investigating specific areas where
he might be able to apply his talents. And Norman never thought
about whether he would be truly happy. He figured happiness, like
other emotional states, is transitory and a byproduct of interest and
activity.

The boys were good students and both gained acceptance to
Twins University, an institution of higher learning dedicated to
educating Twin-Americans. At TU they roomed together, took the
same double major, and dated identical twin sisters. They were two
indistinguishable peas in a pod, except for one thing—the questions
they asked.

Why was I born? Will I be a success? Can I be truly happy? Nathan stayed awake at night thinking about these questions. He also thought about them during the day. Although his professors tried their best to reply to his queries, their rejoinders were ambiguous, which left Nathan extremely dissatisfied.

Norman was not burdened by unanswerable questions. He was too busy researching things such as "What can I do with a liberal arts degree after college?" "How can I improve my performance on the lacrosse team?" and "Is there a place off-campus where I can buy bagels with lox and cream cheese?"

When they graduated, the lads left for the Twin Cities to look for jobs and personal relationships. Nathan had a fairly tough time finding employment and people to hang out with because he was obsessed with finding the answers to "Why was I born?" "Will I be a success?" and "Can I be truly happy?" Norman focused on "Where can I find a nine-hundred-dollar-a-month apartment in this town?" "Is there a gym I can join in the area?" and "How can I get that good-looking girl from HR interested in me?"

Norman found an apartment, a gym, and a relationship (with the girl in HR) within six months of arriving in Minneapolis-Saint Paul. His sibling found himself in three-times-a-week therapy with Dr. Peter Popper, a noted psychiatrist and the head of the Popper Institute for the Promotion of Human Progress.

"Dr. Popper, I'm miserable," Nathan said. "No matter how hard I try, I can't seem to find answers to the questions I have. Specifically, 'Why was I born?' 'Will I be a success?' and 'Can I truly be happy?' Can you help me with my problem?"

Peter Popper picked a peck of pickled peppers from his indoor spice garden and looked to see if there was mold growing on the preserved fruits (which are often incorrectly thought of as vegetables). Satisfied there wasn't, he began to speak. "Nathan, the questions you are preoccupied with are not exact enough that they can be reasonably answered. Let me pose a question to you. Do other members of your family ask questions like yours?"

"No, doctor. As a matter of fact, my brother has an opposite problem. The questions he asks aren't big and important ones like mine. They're small and insignificant questions like 'What's playing tonight at the movies?' and 'Where can I find a bakery in town with good cheesecake?'"

"But, Nathan," Popper proclaimed, "those questions can be dealt with. Your brother can look up movie listings on the internet and ask people in his neighborhood for bakery recommendations. He's not wasting his time asking why he was born; he's too busy living. And he's not consumed with contemplating whether or not he will be a success; he's successfully getting answers to his questions. As for the idea of true happiness, who do you think is happier, you or your sibling?"

"I suppose he is. Norman doesn't complain. He just figures out what to do and does it."

"What happens when something Norman does doesn't work out?"

"He goes back to the drawing board, analyzes what went wrong, and comes up with another plan."

"Your brother is obviously using the scientific method in his daily life—experiment, evaluate, revise if necessary. I recommend that method to all my patients and I am going to recommend it to you."

"Can the scientific method help me to answer 'Why was I born?' 'Will I be a success?' and 'Can I be truly happy?'"

"I'm afraid not," Popper replied. "Such questions are useless to science because they can't be tested. I suggest you concentrate on forming questions that involve taking constructive action. I believe if you do that, you will feel happier and be more successful."

"I think I'll give that idea a shot, doc," Nathan said. "I don't see how it could hurt. I think I'll take some constructive action right now. The woman who comes to see you after I do, is she married?"

"I can't answer that question, Nathan. It's privileged information."

"No problem. I'll just look to see if she's wearing a wedding band and if she's not I'll ask my cousin Gary, who's a gumshoe in Green Bay, to do a background check on her. If it turns out she is single, I'm going to ask her out."

"That's your call, Nathan. I can't advise you one way or another on the matter."

"That's okay, Dr. Popper. I have another question to ask you that involves taking constructive action."

"What's the question, Nathan?"

"I've got a hankering for a Venti iced skinny hazelnut macchiato, sugar-free syrup, extra shot, no whip and a whole wheat cranberry pecan biscotti. Is there a Starbucks around here?"

The Way to San Jose

Sarah Barnhart was a struggling, stressed-out actress obsessed with the question "Is there anything wrong in being different?" She had thought about that question as a teenager, as a woman in her twenties, as a thirty-something, and was thinking about it now as she walked home from a birthday party her parents had just thrown for her. At that party, a celebration of her turning forty-one, her three siblings had given Sarah lots of presents and best wishes for a happy life.

Chip, the eldest child in the family, was a high-level business executive. He had four beautiful children, three Aston Martins, two Lear jets, a trophy wife, and homes all over the world. Biff, the next in line, was a happily married medical doctor and the father of adorable twin boys. Muffy, the third kid, worked as a patent attorney and had an investment banker as a spouse. Sarah, the youngest of the group, lived alone, had no boyfriend, and toiled as an office temp in downtown LA. She wanted to star in feature films but despite having shown up for hundreds of auditions, the closest she had ever come to achieving her goal was to be an extra in a couple of Woody Allen flicks.

Before she left the party, her father had asked Sarah, "When are you going to find a normal job, get married, and settle down? Sarah had muttered something like "I don't know; when the time is right, I suppose." But she hadn't really meant it. She didn't want to lead a regular life and settle down. She wanted to pursue her dream of being a leading lady in the movies.

When Sarah was two blocks from her house, a little green man with large pointed ears and springs for legs bounced up to her and said in a high, squeaky voice, "Do you know the way to San Jose?"

"Isn't that the title of a Burt Bachrach song?" Sarah replied.

"Yes, it is," the lime-colored fellow said. "That song inspired me to visit San Jose thirty years ago."

"Why are you going back there?"

"Because I value conventionality. The Bachrach song talks about an actor who has trouble making it in LA so he decides to return to his roots in San Jose. This led me to think that the people who live in San Jose are less adventurous than the people who reside in Los Angeles. Since the life forms on my planet are not all that daring, I thought San Jose would be the perfect place to travel to. I loved it then and I look forward to seeing it now."

"That's a great story," Sarah said, "worthy of being made into a movie. May I ask you what part of the cosmos you call home?"

"I'm from Congruity, a small planet that is two galaxies and a black hole to the left of your universe. There's a video in my rocket ship that describes where I live. Would you care to see it?"

Sarah thought that might be fun, so she agreed to go with the alien to his spacecraft. When they got to the vehicle, which had been ticketed for having no license plates and being parked in a no-loading zone, they went on board and into a projection room. There the creature put what looked like a DVD into a video player.

The recording began with a voiceover announcement. "Welcome to Congruity, a planet whose inhabitants have identical brains and nervous systems. We think the same, feel the same, and have indistinguishable aims and desires. Our norm is to conform. We applaud alikeness and deplore disparity. We are our brothers' keepers because, for all intents and purposes, we are our brothers."

The video showed identical-looking green people, living in matching green houses, driving analogous green cars, eating interchangeable wedges of green cheese, and using green money of varied denominations. When the video was over the extraterrestrial said, "Each year for one week we are allowed to travel and do our thing.

A friend of mine, who made a trip to earth many years ago, brought the Bachrach song about San Jose back to Congruity. When I listened to it, I got really psyched up to see that city."

Sarah didn't respond to the space wayfarer's remarks. Instead, she took a few moments to think about what she had seen on the video. Then she said, "I thought my siblings were conformists, but they're absolute rebels compared to you guys. My brothers and sister look different, live in different-looking houses, drive different-looking cars, and eat different kinds of foods. The one thing they have in common with the folks on your planet is they use green money with different denominations."

The Congruist smiled and replied, "Of course your siblings are different from us and from each other. That's because, to use a general semantics term, they are *organisms-as-wholes-in environments*, which in simple English means humans have unique nervous systems that sense, feel, think, and do things in distinct ways in different situations. People aren't perfectly congruent. That would go against the natural order of things, whatever that is."

Sarah reflected on the intergalactic visitor's observations. It made her think that being different was an ordinary part of the human condition. She might be a bit more eccentric than her more conventional brothers and sisters, but they were also a bit quirky. Chip's favorite item of clothing was a 1960s leisure suit; Biff thought Mickey Mantle had been a better centerfielder than Willie Mays; and Muffy liked warm beer and cold soup.

"Are you okay?" the interplanetary traveler said to Sarah. "You seem to be lost in thought."

"Couldn't be better," Sarah responded. "I was just thinking how fortunate I am to be an autonomous human being."

"That's nice," the alien replied. "Incidentally, I still have to find the way to San Jose. Got any suggestions?"

"Yeah. Be like the guy in the Bachrach song and give up on your life's dreams and aspirations. Forget about doing something out of the ordinary. Just follow the crowd and do whatever the pack does. When you've done that, for all intents and purposes, you're there."

Faith in Frankland

Not so very long ago, but long ago enough that with the all the atomic weapons in the world the planet should have already been wiped out twelve times over, there lived a woman named Faith who had very little tolerance for people who were not direct in conversation. She wanted people to say what they mean and mean what they say. For Faith, talk was about getting down to basics.

One morning, as Faith was boarding a commuter train to go to work, she accidentally bumped into a young man carrying a briefcase.

"I'm sorry," Faith said. "I hope you're okay."

"Just say you're sorry and move on. You don't have to add anything else."

"Look here," Faith replied, a bit flustered. "I was only trying to be polite."

"It seems to me you were being 'over-polite.' You didn't have to say, 'I hope you're okay.' There was no need to use extra words. Just say what's necessary. That's what we're taught where I come from."

"And where would that be?" Faith asked.

"I'm a native of Frankland."

"I've never heard of Frankland. Is that a country?"

"It's a state-of-mind nation. Franklanders share a four-word philosophy, namely 'get to the point.' I'm John. What's your name?"

"My name is Faith and I totally agree with the idea of getting to the point. Why waste time being roundabout when you express yourself. It's so refreshing to find someone who thinks like me regarding that notion. Where is your mind-state? Is it a long way off?"

"No. It's just ten minutes away by *thoughtmotron*."

"What's a thoughtmotron?"

"It's a machine that transports people via their thoughts. You tell the thoughtmotron where you want to go and it takes you there."

"That's unbelievable! How can a machine do that?"

John handed Faith a card. "Come to the address on this card at 9 a.m. on Saturday and you'll find out."

Faith showed up at the designated time and John let her into an apartment that contained what appeared to be a beauty salon hair dryer positioned over a chair in the middle of a living room. John motioned for Faith to sit in the chair.

"To be conveyed to Frankland you will need to repeat our nation's motto three times after I turn on the thoughtmotron. I will join you there five minutes after you arrive."

"What's the motto?" Faith asked.

"Truth talks, BS walks."

As she waited for John at the Thoughtmotron Arrivals Terminal in Frankland, Faith thought to herself that traveling by thoughtmotron was a lot more efficient than traveling by other forms of transportation. And it was a great savings on gas. Then John appeared.

"I've got to go to work," John said. "You want to come with me?"

"Sure," Faith replied.

A secretary was filing her nails at a desk when they entered John's office.

"Good morning," Faith said to the secretary.

"Not for me," the secretary responded. "I have been given too much work and not enough time to finish it."

"That's the way it is in many offices these days," Faith said. "Unfortunately, there doesn't seem to be much one can do about it."

"That's not true. I could quit, I could try to foist the work off to other people, I could say I'm sick and go home, I could complain to my union, I could . . ."

"That's very interesting," Faith interjected, "but I was just making small talk. I really don't want to know all the options you have in dealing with your situation."

"Then you shouldn't have asked me about it," the secretary said. "Truth talks, BS walks." And with that she went back to filing her nails.

When it was time for lunch, Faith and John went to the company cafeteria where they sat next to Ned, one of John's coworkers.

"I find you very sexy," Ned said to Faith. "I'd like to make love to you tonight."

"That's awfully direct. You don't even know my name."

"What does your name have to do with it? It's your body that turns me on."

"Don't you think you're being a bit pushy, Mack?"

"No, I'm being honest. And my name's not Mack. You seem uptight to me. When was the last time you were with a man?"

Faith turned red. Then she turned to John. "I'd like to eat somewhere else if that's all right with you."

"I want to eat here," John replied.

"Fine, enjoy your lunch. I'm leaving."

Faith exited the building and went onto Frankland Avenue, the main thoroughfare in this kingdom of verisimilitude. There she saw a speaker behind a podium addressing a crowd gathered in front of him.

"My fellow Franklanders, our nation is facing a crisis of immense proportion. We are being sabotaged by indirection and good manners. People are walking around using expressions like 'please,' 'how are you,' and 'have a nice day.' These verbal tics are sickening and a huge waste of time. I propose we double the fines on those who are courteous and well mannered and if a person is caught being polite three times in a row we toss them in jail for a few months."

The crowd applauded and began to chant, "Truth talks, BS walks. Truth talks, BS walks." Faith thought, "I got to get out of Frankland."

"Is there an American embassy around here?" Faith asked a passerby.

"No, the only embassy in town is the one for the Civilized World. It's at the end of the block." Faith headed straight for it.

The Ambassador for the Civilized World listened attentively as Faith spoke about the lack of civility in Frankland.

"What's wrong with these people? They seem like savages to me. I don't want to always know what someone is thinking. I want people to treat me with respect and in a gracious manner. This place is disgusting."

The ambassador replied, "Good manners are a lubricant for good human relations. Without them, friction between human beings can lead to stubbornness and hostility. Unfortunately, the people of Frankland are oblivious to the importance of manners. They think comments like 'How do you do?' or 'How are you?' are superfluous because they are 'mere' figures of speech. But they are wrong. The noted general semanticist S.I. Hayakawa observed that the *togetherness* of talking is the most important element in social conversation; the subject matter is secondary. Unfortunately, Franklanders believe that blurting out whatever is on one's mind is the key to effective communication. We've been trying to convince them this is not so."

"How have you been trying to convince them?" Faith asked.

"The Civilized World has offered Franklanders scholarships to take courses in general semantics, a discipline that teaches that some remarks are not meant to directly inform. Rather, certain forms of language contribute to a social mood and establish rapport. General semantics also emphasizes the importance of delaying one's reaction in situations to bring about harmonious interpersonal exchanges."

"What's been the response to your offer?"

"It's not been very good," the ambassador said. "But we're still working on it."

"Well, I hope you're successful in getting Franklanders to be nicer but I don't want to stay around to see if that happens. I want to go home. Can you help me do that?"

"There is a thoughtmotron session taking place at the embassy tonight," the ambassador replied. "Come back then and I'll facilitate your return to 'civilized life.'"

"Do I have to say 'Truth talks, BS walks' for the thoughtmotron to work?"

"Definitely not. To return to civilization all you have to do is recite Ralph Waldo Emerson's edifying belief that no matter how short life is, there's always time for good manners."

"I'll be glad to say that. And I want to say another thing. I think you have been a most civil, civil servant."

"Thank you," the ambassador replied. "It was a pleasure to have been of assistance. I wish you well on your return trip home and when you arrive there I'd appreciate a favor. Please tweet about your positive experience with our embassy and like us on Facebook. Virtuousness in the virtual world can be pretty hard to come by."

Debbie's Extraterrestrial Adventure

Debbie was a damsel with insufficient stress. She was bored with her job, bored with her boyfriend, bored with her cat, bored with her apartment, bored with her neighborhood, bored with her car, pretty much bored with everything.

One fine spring morning, Debbie decided to reinvigorate her life by changing the people and the circumstances that bored her. In the course of a month she got a new job, a new beau, a new apartment in a new part of town, a new car, a new pet, and a dozen pair of new shoes. But a few months later she was back to square one in terms of her interest in people and things.

Over lunch in her apartment, Debbie shared her displeasure with her best friend, Brenda. "I'm so bored and unhappy," Debbie told Brenda. "I thought when I switched the whole shebang I'd feel more involved with life. But I'm as bored now as I was before I made all my changes. I'm sick and tired of the places and people that populate the earth. I wish I could be on another planet where everyone and everything was exciting."

"I'd like to be on another planet, too," Brenda said. "On my planet, bosses would be nice to their secretaries, guys would treat their dates with respect, and there would be enough seats on the subway so you could have somewhere to sit when you went to work in the morning."

"Very funny, Brenda. I spill my guts out and tell you how fed up and miserable I am and all you do is make jokes. You're really not much of a pal."

"Lighten up, honey," Brenda responded. "I'm just as jaded as you are. If you find a heavenly body where things are constantly jumping, let me know. I'll join you there."

The two women spent the rest of the afternoon chatting and when Brenda finally arose to go home it was close to eight p.m. After bidding her friend goodbye, Debbie looked out her living room window and said to the stars above, "I really want to be somewhere else. If there's a higher power in the universe, please whisk me to another planet." Three minutes later she was on a different planet.

"Oh, my god," Debbie said to no one in particular, "where am I?"

A small, happy-faced man with a rather large head and petite little feet, responded. "Your god, or whoever it was who sent you here, has dropped you on Planet X. As the chief greeter to alien visitors for this celestial orb, I bid you a hearty welcome."

"Thanks very much," Debbie replied. "Do you have a name?"

"I'm called Synar," the pint-sized fellow answered. "What is your designation?"

"My name is Debbie."

"Glad to meet you, Debbie. What can I do for you?

"I made a wish to go to another planet because I was bored with my life back on Earth. Do the residents of your planet ever feel bored with their lives?"

"No one is bored on Planet X. Life is engaging and full of wonders for folks here. Every day is a new adventure."

"That's fantastic," Debbie said. "I would love to know your secret. Can you tell me how you keep from becoming blasé with mundane existence?"

"Of course I can. But first I'd like to tell you something about our 'mundane existence.' The inhabitants of Planet X have a lifespan of approximately half a millennium. We are a monogamous group and have long marriages, typically four hundred years or more. We go to work, like I'm sure the people on your planet do, but we don't flit from job to job. Lifetime employment is the norm for us. I have been a

Planet X greeter for the last three centuries."

"That's incredible, Synar. How do you keep life interesting and adventurous if you're committed to the same person and same vocation for hundreds of years at a stretch?"

"That's easy to answer. We follow what Alfred Korzybski, the originator of general semantics, said, namely: treat the familiar as unfamiliar. Here's how it works. Each morning when I get up I could tell myself, 'Ho hum, the same breakfast of corn flakes, cantaloupe, and coffee that I've consumed for the last hundred years. Boring! And Phoebe, my wife of countless decades: Simply a case of same person, different day. And the job: After three centuries why don't I just phone it in.' How do you think I'd feel if I spoke to myself that way?"

"Bored and depressed, I suppose."

"That's right, Debbie. But by treating the familiar as unfamiliar, I don't feel that way. For example, when I came down to breakfast this morning I was thinking, 'what is it about corn flakes, cantaloupe, and coffee that makes it such a satisfying meal? Is it the ingredients, the way I've been brought up to appreciate such a spread, the fact that I'm a fan of alliteration, or maybe something else?' With respect to my relationship with Phoebe, I am always curious about what's on her schedule, what books she's been reading, whether she has heard any good gossip from the neighbors, and a whole bunch of other things. As for my job, I'm constantly looking for new ways to improve my functioning. I could work on doing that forever and there'd still be room for improvement. We Xers have an inquisitive bent. It helps us stay young and alert to possibilities for personal growth."

"Wow!" Debbie proclaimed. "It seems like I've been looking for excitement in all the wrong places. I've been searching outside myself for adventure when, with a change of attitude, I could have made the most ordinary things interesting. If I ever get back home I'm going to practice that philosophy."

"Would you like to return home?"

"Yes, I would. I feel a bit like Dorothy in *The Wizard of Oz*. I've learned an important lesson about how to act more effectively in the world and now I'd like to go home and put that knowledge to use."

"Well, then you shall go home. Why don't you do what Dorothy did at the end of *The Wizard of Oz*—concentrate real hard and say, 'There's no place like home.' 'There's no place like home.' 'There's no place like home.'"

"Do you think that will work?"

"I have no idea, but I think it's worth a try."

"Okay. Here goes . . ." Three minutes after the last "There's no place like home" Debbie was back in her living room.

"My goodness," she cried, "have I been dreaming or did I just return from Planet X?" Before she could give that question more thought her phone rang. It was Brenda.

"Hi, Debbie. I'm bored as a statue with nothing to think about. Do you have any ideas to help motivate me?"

"I certainly do, Brenda. Come over to my apartment tonight for dinner. I'll make us some food and we'll talk about your problem."

"I'd love to visit but you always prepare the same things, Debbie. Is there any way you could whip up something different, maybe something with a little pizzazz?"

"I'll be glad to, Brenda. I've discovered a new garnish. It's called the X Factor and it's guaranteed to spice up any meal. See you for dinner. And don't forget to bring your appetite."

CPSIA information can be obtained
at www.ICGtesting.com
Printed in the USA
LVHW101524080123
736721LV00004B/348